Praise for *The Agassi Story*:

"Melting pot papa Mike Agassi tells a fascinating tale of his family, confessing that father hasn't always known best."
— Bud Collins, *Boston Globe*/NBC

"Mike Agassi has lived a very interesting life, from his early years growing up in Iran to his immigration to the United States and bringing up his family in Las Vegas. Although there have been many difficult periods throughout his life, he was able to bring himself up from real poverty and hard knocks to where he is today. He writes with such honesty and passion about his personal life and family, it makes for most enjoyable reading. It is truly a heartwarming story."
— Kirk Kerkorian

"I liked Andre the first time I saw him. He was six years old and I was interviewing him while doing a World Championship Tennis telecast in Las Vegas. . . . When Andre was asked what he wanted to do when he grew up, he immediately replied, 'I want to be number one.'"
— Vic Braden, sports educator and author of *Vic Braden's Mental Tennis*

THE
AGASSI
STORY

MIKE AGASSI

WITH

DOMINIC COBELLO
AND
KATE SHOUP WELSH

ECW PRESS

Published by ECW PRESS
2120 Queen Street East, Suite 200, Toronto, Ontario, Canada M4E 1E2

NATIONAL LIBRARY OF CANADA CATALOGUING IN PUBLICATION DATA

Cobello, Dominic
The Agassi story / Dominic Cobello ; with Mike Agassi and Kate Shoup Welsh.

ISBN 1-55022-656-8

1. Agassi, Andre, 1970– 2. Agassi, Andre, 1970– —Family. 3. Agassi, Mike. 4. Agassi family. 5. Tennis players — United States — Biography. I. Agassi, Mike II. Welsh, Kate, 1972– III. Title.

GV994.A43C62 2004   796.342′092   C2004-902547-3

Editor: Tracey Millen
Production and Typesetting: Mary Bowness
Printing: Friesens
All photos courtesy of Mike Agassi, except where noted
Front cover photo: Phillip, Mike, and Rita Agassi
Back cover photo: Mike, Betty, and Andre with newborn Jaden
Dominic Cobello author photo courtesy Grigori Ozerski
Kate Shoup Welsh author photo courtesy Sally Chalex

This book is set in Trajan and Minion

The publication of *The Agassi Story* has been generously supported by the Government of Canada through the Book Publishing Industry Development Program. Canadä

DISTRIBUTION

CANADA: Jaguar Book Group, 100 Armstrong Avenue, Georgetown, ON, L7G 5S4
UNITED STATES: Independent Publishers Group, 814 North Franklin Street,
Chicago, Illinois 60610

PRINTED AND BOUND IN CANADA

ECW PRESS
ecwpress.com

This book is dedicated with love to all my family so that they may understand my feelings and character, and know in their hearts that whatever happened in my life made me who I am today. Wrong or right, good intentions were meant.

ACKNOWLEDGMENTS

Mike

Persistence and determination will bring about rewards that one would never hope to dream of. This book was put together with encouragement, patience, guidance, and vision. Thank you to my wife, Betty, who made all the difference in my life; my children Rita, Phillip, Tami, and Andre; my daughters-in-law Martine and Stephanie; my grandchildren Skylar, Carter, Jaden, and Jaz; my son-in-law-to-be Lobsang; my friend Kirk Kerkorian, who I've known for 40 years and who has been an inspiration to me; Dominic Cobello, who kept me on my toes and who had the vision, emotion, and foresight to complete the book; Kate Shoup Welsh, who interviewed me and challenged me to levels of thinking that I normally wouldn't have had; Jack David and his crew at ECW Press; and all my family, extended family, and friends — this book could not have been made without you.

Special thanks to my loving parents, who did the best they could with what they had, and who watched their children one by one leave Iran for a better future.

Dominic

My biggest thanks go to Mike Agassi, "Manuel Shenorhagal yem," for his generosity, his knowledge of tennis, his full availability to work on the book, and for his belief in me. It was so easy working with you. To Betty Agassi, for her patience and generosity, and for helping Mike during the research process. Without you this book would not have been possible. Tami, Rita, Phillip, and Andre: merci for your support of this book. Special thanks to Kate Shoup Welsh, who I believed would bring out the best of Mike's story. Thank you to my dearest wife, Lisette Amireault, who stood by me during the long years of working on this book. Merci mon amour. To my two lovely children, Valérie and Patrick, who are so proud of their father. To my people at ECW: Publisher Jack David, who loves tennis, and his great staff: Tracey Millen, Kulsum Merchant, and foreign rights agent Bill Hanna. Thanks to Jason Resnick of Universal Studios, who convinced me to write the story before the movie; Drew Nederpelt at Metropol Literary; Courtney Cleaver at Muse Media; and my production staff that made the trip to Vegas so many times and worked so diligently: Patrick Beaulac, Grigori Ozerski, and Phil Pantry on camera; Paul Rudolf on editing; and Guy Fagnant on concept. I also want to thank the people who supported and encouraged me with their friendships: Roger Cox, Vic Braden, Leif Shiras, Dawn Mitchell, Rick Rennert, Jim Scott, Rémy and Ginette Dumay, Marc and Anne Dumay, Ron Weinman, Louis Cayer, Pierre Bouchard, Sébastien Lareau, Katherine Klauber Moulton, Gilles Creamer, Francine Lanthier, Armenian Archbishop Hovnan Derderian, Me. Emilio Monaco, and André Vilder. Thanks to all my family, friends, colleagues, and production staff.

To my late mother and father; thanks to them I have gotten this far. Grazie mamma, grazie papa.

Kate

Thanks first and foremost to Dominic Cobello and Mike Agassi for offering me the opportunity of a lifetime, and for their faith in my abilities as a writer. Likewise, thanks to Jack David, Tracey Millen, and all the talented people at ECW Press for taking on this project. Finally, thanks to my husband, Ian; my daughter, Heidi; and to the rest of my wonderful family, who don't just urge me to follow my dreams, but actually help make it possible for me to do so.

AUTHOR'S NOTE

I first connected with Mike Agassi thanks to Jim Scott, the inventor of the Match Mate ball machine, nearly 10 years ago. I was working on a tennis feature for my show about the machines, and Scott told me that Mike knew more about them than anyone in the United States. "Call him!" Scott urged, and so one day, I did. I was struck immediately by how friendly Mike was. "Come down to Vegas anytime!" he said. I thanked him, but I assumed he was just being polite, and besides, I didn't want to impose.

I'd heard of Mike Agassi, of course. You don't spend half your life in tennis without getting a sense of the genius that is Mike, the way I have. Although I started my career promoting rock concerts and music festivals featuring such groups as The Who, The Animals, Jimi Hendrix, and Johnny and Edgar Winter — and worked with John Lennon and Derek Taylor to organize the 1969 Bed In in Montreal — I soon shifted focus to tennis, which I'd loved since I was 15. In addition to organizing several tennis events in Canada, I had founded Tennis Extra Television in 1990 and had since produced hundreds of tennis-related shows.

About a year after I spoke with Mike on the phone, I set up an interview with David Pate. During his career on the ATP Tour, which lasted just shy of a dozen years, Pate had enjoyed some success — especially in doubles, claiming 18 titles. After retiring from the Tour, Pate bought the tennis concession at Bally's in Las Vegas, and I planned to tape him for a segment on one of my shows. When I arrived, however, I was disappointed to discover that Pate was nowhere to be found.

I was frustrated, to be sure. After all, I'd flown all the way from Montreal, where I live, to Las Vegas to tape the show. But then, the staff at Bally's suggested I interview someone else instead: Rita Agassi, Mike's eldest daughter. Rita worked for Pate, running the women's league and the kids' academy. Frankly, this seemed like a better story than David Pate, so I agreed on the spot. Rita hadn't hit it big on the women's tour, but I knew she was a fine player. Besides, she was Andre's big sister. I suspected she had some interesting things to say, and as it turned out, I was right. The segment was a big success.

Afterward, I decided to call Mike and let him know I'd met his daughter. I wasn't sure he still remembered me, but he received my call amiably. "Where are you?" he asked. I told him I was in Vegas. "Come over!" he insisted. So I did. When I arrived at his home, Mike greeted me warmly, and within minutes our talk turned to the game that had captured both our hearts: tennis. We talked and talked and talked. He showed me the ball machines he had famously modified to throw every shot imaginable with tremendous pace, and the foyer filled with trophies that his children had won.

That was the beginning of a wonderful friendship.

In the ensuing years, I visited Mike in Vegas several times, sometimes bringing my cameraman to tape what Mike said about his life. The more I learned about Mike, the more I began to believe that Mike's story deserved to be told to someone other than me. Finally, about three years ago, I thought I'd see if Mike agreed with me.

"Mike," I asked. "What would you say to making a film about your life?"

He sniffed. "Why? Nobody wants to hear about my life," he replied simply.

Despite his reaction, I asked him for permission to pitch the film. It took some cajoling, but I finally convinced Mike that many people would like to know more about him. I began putting out some feelers, first with Stephen Bronfman, who was a friend of my buddy André Lemaire, the director of tennis at Mont Tremblant. In Montreal, Bronfman is about as close to royalty as you can get. After making a killing smuggling booze to the lower 48 during Prohibition, the Bronfman family parlayed a significant percentage of its substantial assets into media holdings. Bronfman referred me to his sister, Ellen, who, with her husband, runs a production company in London. I contacted her, but with no immediate success.

Down but not discouraged, I focused my efforts on making contacts in New York, to no avail. Then, Samantha Deans, who, in addition to being a friend of mine is the principal organizer of many film festivals (including the Film Festival of Montreal), referred me to some of her top contacts. I placed countless calls in Miami, New York, and Los Angeles. But of the 34 studios I contacted, only six replied — including Jason Resnick from Universal. We spoke via phone, and I sent him an early draft of *The Agassi Story* that I had written — for better or worse — myself. He loved it, but noted he'd like to see a finished book before moving forward.

It was back to the drawing board for me.

I returned to Vegas to visit Mike.

"Never mind about the movie," I said. "We're doing a book first."

Mike was a bit surprised. "I didn't know you were serious!" he exclaimed. I assured him that indeed I was, and suggested we sign a contract to seal the deal. And that's how I gained not just a friend, but a business partner — and the opportunity to create an incredible book.

Contract in hand, I began contacting publishers in the U.S. and Canada. I received very positive feedback — everyone could see we had a winner on our hands — and the book was picked up by ECW Press in Toronto.

Which is how it came to be that you're reading this right now. Thanks to ECW, Mike's story — a story about love and family and the American Dream — can now be told.

Enjoy.

Dominic Cobello

"(My dad) was convinced if my eyes were going to move around as a little baby, I might as well be looking at a tennis ball."

— Andre Agassi

INTRODUCTION

B elieve me, I know what it feels like to be on the outside. I've spent the better part of my life on the fringes.

I was born in Persia — later called Iran — in 1930 to Armenian parents, a Christian in an overwhelmingly Muslim country.

I remained an outsider in America, where I emigrated at age 21 with almost no money and even less English.

My outsider status was cemented when, years later, my kids began playing competitive tennis. To the other parents, I was an appallingly middle-class Armenian casino worker from Las Vegas by way of Tehran, trying to involve my kids in the ultimate upper-class sport.

Today, however, I am on the *inside*.

I have an all-access pass to the 2002 Men's Finals of the U.S. Open at Arthur Ashe stadium, a match in which my son Andre is competing against his long-time rival, Pete Sampras.

My wife, Betty, who I met in June of 1959 and married two months later, is with me, along with Andre's wife, tennis legend Steffi Graf, and their son, Jaden. Seated in one of the luxury boxes, among the best seats in the house, we are nervous, as though we are the ones expected to face Pete on this perfect September Sunday in New York.

Today's sky is as blue as it was nearly a year ago, when, mere miles from here, two planes piloted by terrorists demolished the World Trade Center. Predictably, in the aftermath of that disaster, security at the stadium is as tight as Fort Knox; even so, more than 23,000 people have descended upon the National Tennis Center in Flushing Meadows to watch what promises to be a match for the ages.

Before long, the stadium will be in shadow, but for now, the brilliant green court gleams and the white lines that mark the playing area practically vibrate with light. It's a far cry from the dirt courts of my youth, at the American Mission Church in Tehran where I frequently spied American G.I.s and missionaries playing with their British counterparts. I can't say why, but the game fascinated me, and I watched them play whenever I could. There was no fence around the two courts, so any time I saw a ball go astray, I'd chase it down in exchange for some candy or chewing gum at the end of the session. Later, I began tending the courts — pressing and cleaning them, and watering them by hand. Finally, sensing my interest, or perhaps to reward me for all my hard work, one of the regulars, an American G.I., gave me a tennis racket of my own. I used it to learn the fundamentals of the game. No one played with me, but I hit the ball against a wall to develop my strokes. Although I later shifted my focus to boxing, twice representing Iran in the Olympics, it was tennis that had captured my imagination.

The crowd's hum swells to a roar as Andre and Pete emerge from the bowels of the stadium. Andre walks purposefully to the court — he has a tennis walk, slightly pigeon-toed, with short, choppy steps — and begins warming up, shuffling through his deck of strokes. He hits quickly, while the ball is still on the rise, and *hard* — you half expect his return to knock the racket from Pete's hands. Everything about Andre's swing — that exaggerated looped back-swing, the way he finishes with his weight on his back foot — contradicts traditional tennis teaching, but it works. He puts his whole body into each stroke, snapping his hip and wrist like a slingshot, generating tremendous torque and power, exactly the way I taught him to when he was barely old enough to walk.

Andre, the youngest of my four children, wasn't the first kid I tried to coach. That dubious honor goes to my oldest child, Rita. She was amazing. Headstrong and feisty, Rita had an unbelievable two-handed weapon on both sides, and could hit a tennis ball almost as hard as Andre does. The fact is, though, I ruined tennis for Rita by pushing her too hard.

I made the same mistake with my second child, Phillip, who had a tremendous game, but who lacked that killer instinct. In other words, he's about the nicest guy you could ever hope to meet, always putting himself out for others.

Fortunately, by the time my third child, Tami, was born, I'd wised up — at least a bit. I didn't push her the way I did Rita and Phillip. I taught her to play, of course, but I gave her the freedom to pursue other interests. That's probably why, of all my kids, I suspect that Tami is the happiest, the most well adjusted.

I learned a lot by coaching Rita, Phillip, and Tami, so by the time Andre was born on April 29, 1970, nearly 10 years after Rita's arrival, I was ready. I decided that I wouldn't push him the way I had Rita and Phillip, but I would begin teaching him about tennis at a very early age. I figured if he took to the game, then we would take it from there.

As it turned out, Andre wasn't just the most talented of my four kids, he was the most willing. He had the desire. I don't know if it was the desire to play tennis or if it was simply the desire to please me, but he had it. Whenever Andre found a free moment — before school, after school, you name it — he was on the tennis court, practicing his strokes for hours at a time.

Andre and Pete begin their match, and the crowd murmurs appreciatively at the thwack of the ball, at the grunts of the players. But with Pete's serve-and-volley game trumping Andre's baseline strategy, my son quickly finds himself down two sets to one, and I fight to quell my frustration. I taught Andre to play a serve-and-volley game, but my teachings were undermined by the man who later coached Andre, Nick Bollettieri.

I sent Andre to Bollettieri after seeing a spot on *60 Minutes* about Bollettieri's tennis academy in Bradenton, Florida. I'd heard of Bollettieri before — I'd even met him once on the courts of the Tropicana Hotel in Las Vegas, where I once worked as a teaching pro — and knew that he ran a very strict program. But it wasn't Bollettieri's drill-sergeant persona that interested me; rather, it was the simple fact that the academy boasted dozens of kids who played a mean game of tennis.

In Las Vegas, where I'd finally settled after immigrating to Chicago from Iran, finding players who could really challenge Andre was extremely difficult. At Bollettieri's, however, there were any number of kids who could challenge Andre enough that he could continue to improve. And so, at the age of 13, Andre moved to Florida to attend school and train with Nick full time.

For Andre, life at the academy was hard, but he remained there until turning pro at 16. And because he was loyal, Andre kept Nick as his coach even after he left Bradenton. There was just one problem: Bollettieri had, in my view, wrecked Andre's game. Andre went from a kid who played serve-and-volley tennis, who could nail every shot in the book, to a kid who camped out on the baseline. Although Andre has undoubtedly been a major force in American tennis — and certainly one of the best to ever play the game — I contend he would have been an even stronger player had he retained his original style, the style I taught him.

Even so, Andre did see success on the tour, and with each win, Nick's reputation — and by extension, his academy — grew. But in 1993, after nearly 10 years as Andre's coach, Bollettieri abruptly resigned, claiming he hadn't been fairly compensated for his work. Instead of informing Andre of his decision in person, Bollettieri sent him a letter, and leaked the news to a reporter first. Andre was devastated.

As Andre battles Sampras in the fourth set, I glance at Steffi. I like this girl. Arguably the best female tennis player ever, and feared by her competitors for her fierce forehand, Steffi retired from the game in 1999, after racking up an incredible 22 Grand Slam titles. If anyone can understand the pressures Andre faces, if anyone can comprehend what Andre is trying to achieve, it is Steffi.

Which is why Steffi looks torn as she watches Andre's match, like she can't decide whether to curl up in the corner from the sheer stress of watching Andre play or to storm the court and finish the match herself — a task for which she is uniquely qualified, having won this tournament an unbelievable five times. And Steffi, like Andre, is crushed when Sampras finally serves for the win. We were sure Andre would win today, just as he won this tournament in 1994 and again in 1999, just months after he and Steffi started dating. We saw it in his eyes, in his swagger. But today, Sampras is just better.

As Andre gracefully shakes hands with his opponent, I sense that people around me are watching to see how I will react. After Andre won his first Grand Slam tournament, Wimbledon in 1992, I failed to congratulate him, and instead asked why he dropped the fourth set. (In truth, that was a bit of a misunderstanding; I only meant to say that he could have won in four sets, not five. I was making an observation, not passing judgment.) But I have learned a few things since then, most notably that these days, Andre can be trusted to always do his best — something he didn't always do — which is really all I ever wanted from him.

Nonetheless, I know I have a reputation. I'm the crazy Iranian from Las Vegas who browbeat his kids into mastering tennis. I'm the one with outlandish theories on how the game should be played.

People say I'm abrasive. Domineering. Fanatical. Overbearing. Obnoxious. Temperamental. Aggressive. Overzealous.

I've been called a "hectoring bully," a "brutal taskmaster," and a "psycho tennismonger," whatever that is. I am considered by many to be intimidating, disruptive, destructive, and abusive. I am generally lumped into that fraternity of insufferable tennis fathers, alongside other pariahs like Stefano Capriati, Jim Pierce, Damir Dokic, Marinko Lucic, and Richard Williams (who, incidentally, I quite like). Then again, I defy you to find a top-ten player who *wasn't* driven, at first anyway, by at least one of his parents.

People say I pushed my kids too hard, that I nearly destroyed them. And you know what? They're right. I was too hard on them. I made them feel like what they did was never good enough. But after the childhood I had, fighting for every scrap in Iran, I was determined to give my kids a better life. However misguided I may have been, I pushed my kids because I loved them.

The fact is, what we did was more difficult than hitting the Megabucks jackpot, and the real sacrifice was Andre's — was *all* of my kids' — childhood.

But this, too, is true: It was worth it.

Every father has a dream for his children, and will do anything to make that dream a reality. Some people want their child to be a doctor. Some people want their child to be president. I wanted my kids to be world-champion tennis players.

And with Andre, my dream — and, I believe, I *hope*, his dream — came true.

CHAPTER ONE

"Better to go from poverty to riches than from riches to poverty."
— Chinese proverb

I am happy in this house. Really, I am.

Nestled in the crook of the curve where Andre Drive pours into Agassi Court (I petitioned the city to rename our streets), it's a big, beautiful home, about 5,000 square feet, bright, airy, open, and filled with a lifetime of things that my wife, my kids, and I have accumulated. Unkempt rows of family photos — the smiling faces of my four children and of my four grandchildren — perch on the mantle. A riot of trophies occupies the foyer. The kitchen boasts two refrigerators, which, together, store enough food to feed a Division I football team. There are — drum roll, please — *five* bathrooms. (You'll understand their significance in a moment.) Out back is a beautiful enclosed tennis court, one of the finest in town.

Moving here was a big decision for me. When my youngest son, Andre, told me he'd bought four lots on the western outskirts of town, that he was going to build a tennis court, a health spa, and two houses there, and that one of those houses was meant for me and Betty, I said thanks, but no thanks.

"Why?" he demanded. It was 1993, the year after he'd won Wimbledon for the first time.

Why? Lots of reasons. For one, I'd spent the last 20 years tweaking our old house on Tara Street to make it just right. I paid $120,000 for it in 1973 and spent an additional $180,000 over the years on improvements. (In 1973, Tara Street was practically in the middle of the desert. I used to call Betty a dozen times a night when I was working to make sure bandits hadn't taken over the place. Now, though, the neighborhood has been swallowed up by the growing blob that is Las Vegas.) The house was stucco when we bought it, and I bricked it from the bottom up. I added a storage room, a three-car carport, and space for two extra cars in the garage. I extended the walls around the house and added an iron fence. And of course, in 1974, I built a tennis court in the backyard using special dirt and denser-than-usual concrete to prevent cracking. Plus, the house was paid for; my only real expenses were taxes, insurance, and utilities. At the new house, we'd have to pay a monthly association fee of $300 — it was like paying rent!

"Don't worry about it," Andre said. "I'll pay the association fee. You won't pay a cent."

But I was a proud person. I didn't want my son to buy me a house; he'd already bought me a car, a Cadillac, and even that seemed extravagant. I appreciated that Andre wanted to share the wealth he'd accumulated during his years on the pro circuit, but in all truth, I never wanted that wealth for myself. Besides, I had plenty of money of my own. I'd spent the last 30 years working in various Las Vegas casinos, and planned to spend the next 30 years doing more of the same. If I wanted a new house, I'd buy one myself.

My wife, however, had other ideas. She wanted to move, and

there it was. I was outvoted. So we came here, and built the tennis court right away; everything I had on Tara Street, I had here, plus a little more. Once I got over feeling uncomfortable accepting such a large gift from Andre, once I settled into our new home, I was fine.

I didn't thank him; I hadn't wanted the house in the first place. But I was fine.

My house in Las Vegas is plotted in a walled community. To enter, you must pass a sentried gate; part of me is always a little surprised when the guard lets me through. You see, this house, this neighborhood, could not be more different from the one in which I grew up.

In Tehran, where I was born in 1930, I ate, slept, *lived* with my mother, father, three brothers, and sister in a room barely 15-by-20 feet. There was no space for a dinner table, so we ate seated on the dirt floor; after each meal, Father, who passed his days toiling as a carpenter, read to us from the Bible. We had no radio. We did have a single bicycle — the kind with a basket on the back — for the whole family, which we used primarily to travel to and from the marketplace. Wearing shirts Mother had sewn and socks she had knitted, we slept two by two on mattresses she made by hand, pushing them up against the wall each morning only to pull them out again each night.

My family's room was part of a larger walled compound, which we shared with several other families — about 35 people in all. The compound itself, located in the heart of Tehran, was square in shape with a courtyard in the middle and surrounded by towering walls that offered street access through a single door. There was no electricity, no running water. We shared a single toilet — more like a hole in the ground — with our neighbors. (Do you see why I'm fired up about having five bathrooms now?) No matter what time of day it was, there was always a line for the facilities, which is why the men frequently practiced their aim on the compound's interior walls. If we were lucky, in addition to our daily sponge baths, we cleaned up once a week at the local communal bathhouse. It sounds horrible, I know. But it really wasn't. We looked out for our neighbors — among them several Jews, some Armenians, and some native Persians — and they looked out for us, skirmishes for bathroom privileges notwithstanding.

Needless to say, the compound did *not* have a tennis court.

You have to wonder, then, how a guy like me fell in love with a game like tennis. After all, Tehran wasn't exactly a tennis mecca, despite its hospitable climate. And even if it had been, my family was hardly of a class that played the game. In those days, Persian society was strictly divided into tiers, or *tabagheh*, and as Christian Armenians, we Agassis existed solidly on the bottom.

My father, David Agassi, was a quiet man, strongly built, very religious, and I adored him. He was born during the 1880s to Armenian parents in Kiev. (Our original family name was Agassian, which, thanks to the "ian" at the end, clearly identified us as Armenian. As a skin-saving measure during a time when the Turks frequently used Armenians for target practice, an industrious ancestor changed the family name to Agassi.) He married, fathered two sons, and built a thriving carpentry business — he was among the first to use the tongue-in-groove technique for laying floors — but lost it all after the 1918–1920 war between the White Russians and the Communists.

To say that Kiev, which is part of the Ukraine, was a hotbed of political activity during that time would be a gross understatement. After optimistically declaring its independence from Russia in early 1918, the Ukraine changed hands three times — it was overrun once by the Germans and twice by the Bolsheviks, who, as the Red Army, fought under the banner of Communism — before being conquered in 1919 by the White Army, in which my father had enlisted.

The White Army consisted primarily of the newly alienated Russian gentry: land holders whose property had been confiscated by Bolsheviks, factory owners whose plants had been nationalized. As a prosperous businessman, my father fit right in. The group's basic platform was "Down with Communism," but its leadership offered little in the way of alternative political or economic programs. This oversight, plus persistent military blunders, personal rivalries, and an inability to coordinate its leadership, made the group an easy target for the highly organized Red Army — which explains why the success of the White Army in the Ukraine was short-lived. In December of 1919, the area was, yet again, conquered by the Red Army; this time, it was for keeps.

The Communists' victory spelled disaster for my father. The loss of his fortune, which he had cobbled together during a lifetime of work, was a foregone conclusion. And although his life had been spared by the Bolsheviks, he felt certain it was simply a matter of time before he, like so many of the men with whom he had served, faced the firing squad. So, leaving behind his wife and two sons, who refused to move, and his prosperous business, my father scrambled for the Russo-Persian border — first on a bicycle and later by mule and bus — making a beeline for Tehran.

Why Tehran? I can't be sure. Europe was a lot closer, but perhaps he thought his odds were better crossing the desert. Or maybe my father knew that in those days, Persia was the destination for many refugees, chief among them his fellow Armenians. They poured into the desert from their ancestral homeland in Turkish Armenia — many without food or water — after the Turks issued an edict in 1916 demanding the extermination of all Armenians living in the Ottoman Empire, with no regard to "age or sex, nor to conscientious scruples." As many as two million Armenians died in this campaign; many who survived fled to Europe, Asia, and some to Persia's capital, Tehran, an immense city on the shores of the Caspian Sea, where they could reasonably hope to find work.

My mother, Noonia, who was born in Turkish Armenia, had also made the journey to Tehran, though she never attributed it to the Armenian genocide as such. By her telling, she visited Tehran with her family, met my father, and decided to stay. Although he was much older than she was, by 20 years or so, they married and soon started a family of their own. Together they had five children: my brother Issar, born in 1925; my brother Samuel, born in 1927; me, who they called Emmanuel, born on December 25, 1930; my sister Helen, born in 1933; and my baby brother Helmut, born during World War II, named for a kindly German neighbor who had been deported from Iran during the war.

It is sometimes difficult for Westerners to understand that the Iran of my youth was not the hostile, dangerous, repressive place it is now. Today's Iran is governed by the laws of a madman — the late Ayatollah Khomeini, who seized power in 1979 — and his followers.

Women who once enjoyed some of the most progressive social policies in the Middle East are now prohibited from showing their hair in public because, according to one former Iranian leader, it "emits rays that drive men insane." Those who don't comply receive 74 lashes.

Today, Iran is a place where adulterers are stoned, where lucky dissenters are jailed and unlucky ones are executed, where decent people live in fear. It's a place where the press is considered "free" as long as it publishes material in accordance with Islamic principles, where books espousing unsanctioned viewpoints are burned. Iran's poor get poorer, and there are few opportunities — Iran's oil-based economy has remained stagnant since the overthrow of the shah in 1979 — and even less hope.

Each whisper of uprising only tightens the shackles. Iran's mullahs use their control of the police and the courts to silence dissenters, and the Guardian Council, an unelected body that is dominated by clerics, regularly vetoes reform legislation and even excludes less-conservative parliamentary candidates from the electoral ballot — a privilege it exercised as recently as early 2004.

It was not always so. My Iran, or Persia, was at least on the road to modernization, although it had not yet arrived. Our king, or *shah*, Reza Shah Pahlavi, envisioned a Persia modeled after the more advanced nations of Europe — that is, one that was economically and culturally strong, one that was centrally governed, one that was sovereign, and one that was influential in regional affairs. To this end, he built an army 125,000 strong; overhauled the government's administrative and bureaucratic processes; reorganized the treasury; created an extensive secular school system based upon the French model and established a European-style university in

Tehran; expanded Persia's network of roads and completed the Trans-Iranian railroad; and spearheaded the creation of several state-owned factories to produce basic consumer goods — textiles, matches, canned goods, sugar, cigarettes, and the like. In an effort to strengthen the nation's cultural identity, he persuaded all countries with which Persia had diplomatic ties to call our country by its name in Farsi, "Iran."

The socially progressive Reza Shah also enacted sweeping cultural changes, imposing European dress on the Iranian population and establishing a meritocracy. Under his reign, the importance of inherited wealth or family connections was diminished; instead, Reza Shah, himself a self-made man, emphasized competence and performance and dismissed any officials found lacking. Perhaps most impressive, he allowed women to enter schools and the workforce — a maneuver practically unheard of in that region of the world, even today. The rights of women would be extended under Reza Shah's son, Mohammad Reza Shah Pahlavi, who, in 1963, granted them the right to vote.

Of course, I'm not so naïve as to think that the Iran of my youth was a Utopian society. Although Reza Shah and, later, Mohammad Reza Shah were responsible for widespread reform, these successes were dampened by their dictatorial governing style. They hamstrung the country's parliament, or *Majlis*; they muzzled the press; and employing their secret police force, called the SAVAK, they arrested their opponents. Whole pockets of the populace — including us, because we were Christians — were not permitted to vote. The Pahlavis' tax policies, which overburdened the lower class, didn't endear them to Iran's rank-and-file citizenry, and of course, there were immense inequities in the distribution of wealth, as evidenced by our own living situation as compared to the rich lifestyle of the Pahlavis.

When I was about six years old, I saw first-hand just how lavishly the Pahlavis lived. Because of his reputation as a fine carpenter, my father had been hired by Reza Shah to lay flooring and to build a winding oak staircase in the Green Palace. One day, he brought me and my brother Issar along on the job.

After walking from our compound to the palace — a distance of about five miles — soldiers guarding the grounds let us pass, and we followed my father inside. It seemed like *everything* was made of marble, and anything that wasn't, was constructed of dark, beautiful wood. Suspended from the great ceiling were chandeliers from all over the world — Italy, India, Mexico, you name it. One room was covered entirely in silver mirrors. Resting on my father's beautiful floors were dining tables the length of bowling lanes. And the grounds! Spectacular. The palace was surrounded by forests, springs, gardens, greenhouses, pools, lagoons, and playgrounds, which you navigated via a series of tree-covered avenues. Not that I walked those avenues myself, mind you; the word was, the shah was learning to shoot, and anything that moved was fair game. Worried that the king might shoot one of us — either unwittingly or for sport — my brother and I stayed close by my father as he worked.

Although Iran declared its neutrality at the outbreak of World War II, it was nevertheless raided by Britain and the U.S.S.R. in August of 1941 — partly because of the shah's refusal to expel German nationals from the country, but more importantly because the

Allies needed access to the Trans-Iranian railroad to transport sup-plies and troops into the Soviet Union. Reza Shah's armed forces, thought to be formidable, proved a colossal disappointment. Within three days, the Soviets and the British had decimated the Iranian Army, Air Force, and Navy.

The Allies forced Reza Shah to abdicate (he died in exile in 1944), but did permit his son, 21-year-old Mohammad Reza Shah Pahlavi, to succeed the throne — the beginning of a reign that would endure for nearly 40 years. In January 1942, Iran agreed to provide non-military support to the Allies; in September 1943, Iran would go so far as to declare war on Germany itself — amazing, when you consider that Reza Shah had at one time been friendly with Hitler, and that Germany had been Iran's most important trading partner prior to the war. The expulsion of German nationals from Iran followed.

Like most countries involved in the war effort, food and other necessities in Iran were scarce, and people like us — that is, people in the lower class — struggled mightily thanks to severe inflation. For my family, though, that wasn't the half of it. Reza Shah had been ousted by the Allies before he got around to paying my father for his work at the Green Palace. Years of work — those beautiful floors, that graceful staircase — all for nothing. It just about killed him.

On the plus side, from my point of view anyway, wartime in Tehran meant a spike in the number of American and British sol-diers — nearly 150,000 in all — many of whom gave me candy on a regular basis. We'd always had British soldiers in Tehran, thanks to Great Britain's interest in Iranian oil, but the Americans were new — and, I discovered, very generous. On one occasion, an American soldier, appalled by my holey shoes, gave me a new pair of boots. The soldiers taught us kids some choice English words; the first one I learned was "victory," like Churchill, "V for victory."

When these soldiers weren't relegated to duties at camp — where, incidentally, my brother Sam worked recharging the batteries and generators that died en route to Tehran, and where we once saw Bob Hope perform — they gravitated to the American Mission Church in Tehran, which, it so happens, was the very church our family attended thanks to its close proximity to our home. In my family, we were born in the church. We *believed*. Every Sunday without fail we attended the Armenian sermon at 7:00 a.m., followed by the Persian one at 9:00 a.m. My siblings and I went to Sunday school, and I sang in the choir.

The church, itself part of an enormous walled compound — I'd say seven blocks by seven blocks — was run by Presbyterian missionaries from the United States who delivered sermons in Armenian, Persian (the official language of Iran, also called Farsi), and English. The church's heavily treed grounds accommodated several soccer fields and a picnic area. Numerous terra-cotta brick buildings housed a pediatric clinic, several homes for the American missionaries and their families, a school for English-speaking foreigners attended by the missionaries' children as well as by the children of people who worked at the American and British embassies, another school in which lessons were taught in Persian (which I attended), and a smattering of chapels — one for Persian services, one for Armenian services, and one for English services. In each chapel, a towering ceiling sheltered the church's cool interior from the blazing heat outside, although colored sunlight did stream in through the stained-glass windows, warming the gleaming, polished pews that my father had built with his own two hands.

The church complex was made even more popular among American and British soldiers by the two tennis courts located within the compound walls. Although the courts were made of dirt and lacked fences, they saw tremendous use, especially during the war. The men who played at the mission weren't very good, but they played hard and laughed often.

For me, it was love at first sight. Until then, my game had been soccer, which I played barefoot. And of course, like most boys I knew, I'd engaged in my share of street fights. But something about tennis piqued my interest like nothing ever had, something I can't quite define. I loved the thwack of the ball, the arc of a well-played stroke. I loved the sheen of the wooden racket, the twang of the steel-wire strings. I loved the almost infinite variability of the game, the way you rarely saw the *exact* same shot twice. Lying on my mattress at night or walking to school with my brothers, I sifted through the game in my mind, analyzing why the ball behaved the way it did, dissecting the techniques players used to make it behave differently.

After church, after school, or whenever I had a spare moment, I watched those soldiers play, and whenever a ball went astray, I chased it down in exchange for some candy or chewing gum. Before long, I gladly assumed the responsibility of maintaining the courts, pressing them with a heavy roller, sweeping them clean, and watering them to pack down the dirt. In Tehran, we didn't have piped-in water. Instead, water flowed downward from Mount Damavand (located on the outskirts of town), through the city's gutters, which acted like aqueducts, and into underground hand-made tanks or into small reservoirs or pools. So anytime I watered the court, I had to climb down to one of the tanks, open the valve, fill the bucket, close the valve, climb back up, lug the bucket to the court, and pour it onto the dirt, over and over, until the job was done. (If I was in a hurry, I would take water from a nearby pool, which was a bit easier.) I nailed down the tape that served as the line, and painted it with chalk water. It sounds brutal — tending two dusty courts under the piercing Persian sun, lugging heavy buckets of water around — but for me it was a delightful job, and I was happy to do it.

I have never minded working hard.

One day, one of the regulars, an American G.I., handed me his racket. "This is for you," he said.

I was floored. The racket was a homely thing, all chipped wood and steel-wire strings, but I was so thrilled to have it, so excited, that I *literally* jumped for joy. Although I didn't know enough English to thank the G.I. properly, I think he got the message. Afterward, I used a ball that had been left behind to hit against the church wall before running home to show the racket to my parents.

"Look!" I beamed, thrusting the racket into my father's hands.

He looked it over, and then asked me sternly, "Who gave this to you?"

"One of the soldiers at the mission," I said, still breathless with excitement.

"What does he want in return?" My father was very protective, and conscious of some of the uglier aspects of Iranian life — namely, the frequency with which young boys were molested in our area.

I told my father I didn't think the soldier wanted anything in return, but the next time we went to the church, my father still sought out the American major. In halting English, he asked, "Why did you give the racket to my son?"

The American was taken aback. "He has helped us," he answered. "Anytime we come to play, he is here."

Satisfied, my father let me keep the racket.

I kept it until I left for America a decade later.

CHAPTER TWO

"Ask me about the Olympics, and I'll tell you there is nothing greater."
— Andre Agassi

I sat overlooking Center Court of the Stone Mountain Park Tennis Center for Andre's gold-medal match during the 1996 Olympic Games in Atlanta, one of the few times I'd ever watched Andre play in person during his pro career. (I usually prefer to watch his matches on satellite television from the comfort of my living room.) The stadium was a madhouse, filled almost entirely with Americans who were chanting and cheering for Andre. I was sitting pretty far up, away from the television cameras, with my elder son, Phillip; with Andre's girlfriend, Brooke Shields; and with several of Andre's friends from Las Vegas. Andre had sent his plane to collect us the previous day, and we'd had a nice flight. It was fun. After a rain-delayed start, the blistering Atlanta sun emerged, and Andre came out swinging against two-time French Open champion Sergi Bruguera, a Spaniard.

Not many of the top players had come to that Olympiad. It's tough when the Olympics fall too close to Wimbledon and the French Open, and that year they did. But Andre participated anyway because, well, they asked him to. It was the first time he'd been asked. Besides, the Olympics are the only event in tennis where you truly represent your country. In Davis Cup, they act like you're representing America when you're really representing the USTA, but that's a whole other story. Truly representing America was important to Andre.

But that wasn't all. There was another reason Andre found the Olympics compelling.

When he was 16, Andre discovered something about me that I'd kept from him, from all my kids: I twice competed in the Olympics as a boxer. So when, during the course of an interview, a reporter asked Andre about my Olympic career, he was flummoxed.

"Why didn't you tell us?" he demanded afterward.

The fact was, I'd kept my athletic past a secret from my kids because I didn't want to put any ideas in their heads. I never wanted them to box, to put their faces in front of a punch. I was worried that if they knew about my career as a fighter, they might decide to take to the ring themselves, the way Laila Ali and Jacqui Frazier did. Besides, it just wasn't important to me that they know.

I could tell after the first set, which Andre won 6–2 in a mere 19 minutes, that the contest was pretty one-sided. As it turned out, Bruguera captured only six games the entire match, which Andre won in three sets. An hour later, I watched my son mount the platform, listened to the national anthem, gazed at the American flag descending from the rafters, and saw him receive his gold medal.

I was very proud. For me, it was the biggest win of Andre's career. Bigger than Wimbledon in 1992, bigger than the U.S. Open in 1994.

When the ceremony was over, I went over to him and touched the medal. "This is the closest I will ever come to a gold medal," I said, beaming, my voice cracking with emotion. I might have even cried a little. The way I saw it, it didn't matter whether he won it or I won it; *we* won it. That was the most important thing.

We hugged. Some people took our pictures. But then I walked away and left him alone because it wasn't my day; it was his day.

My chance at an Olympic medal of my own had long since come and gone.

It didn't take a rocket scientist to figure out that I didn't have much of a future as a tennis player, but it wasn't for lack of trying. If I had a dollar for each hour I spent hitting against the wall at the American Mission Church, I'd have enough cash to buy out the MGM Grand. I spent an eternity experimenting, trying to grasp the fundamentals of the game, to replicate shots I'd seen.

The problem was I didn't have anyone to practice with. None of the kids in the neighborhood had a racket. And the soldiers and missionaries, generous as they were, weren't particularly jazzed about hitting around with a 13-year-old novice whose grasp of English was even worse than his grasp of tennis. Given my family's financial situation, hiring a coach was not an option. Plus, I didn't exactly have top-notch equipment, and buying better stuff was out of the question. Don't get me wrong, I treasured the racket I'd received from that kindly American G.I., but it wasn't exactly a catgut-and-titanium affair.

Fortunately for me, I *did* have a future as a fighter.

Even as a young boy, I engaged in a fair number of street fights. It seems strange now; street fighting just isn't done anymore, unless you're some kind of low-class hooligan. But in those days, in

Tehran anyway, it was just something we did to pass the time, the way kids today skateboard or play street hockey. I am hard-pressed to remember just what, exactly, we were fighting about, but fight we did, primarily with children from neighboring streets. I discovered that I was an exceptionally good fighter, very quick, with a powerful punch. Any time I felt threatened . . . *bam!*

Apparently, I still pack that punch; Betty says I sometimes wallop her in my sleep, when I'm dreaming about boxing.

It didn't occur to me that fighting could be lucrative, however, until the Russian circus came to town. As one of the acts, two men entered the ring and whaled away at each other for a while; afterward, the ring master held up some gloves and challenged anybody from the crowd to take their shot at a share of the purse. I thought, "Gosh, I wish I was bigger! I wish I was older! I would take him!"

That got me interested.

One day, when I was about 16, after a particularly nasty scuffle in which I remained standing but my opponents did not, a man approached me.

"You," he said to me after the crowd had dispersed. "You could be a very good boxer."

Naturally, I was suspicious. My father's efforts to protect us from strangers weren't entirely lost on me. I nodded politely at the man and began to turn away, but he continued. "I'm a trainer at the Nerou Rastey club."

This got my attention. Nerou Rastey was a beautiful private club in the heart of Tehran. And so, when the man invited me to check the place out, I accepted.

We walked there together, and he escorted me inside. The space was crammed with equipment for weight lifting, wrestling, and gymnastics, plus a ping-pong table and a junior basketball court, smaller than regulation size. On one side of the main floor were a boxing ring and a punching bag. The club's owner, a woman (her husband had died and left her the business), lived in an apartment upstairs.

The trainer led me to the ring, where he laced some gloves over my fists. Then he threw me to the wolves. My first opponent gave me a bloody nose, but I managed to knock him out soon thereafter. Someone else challenged me, and quickly met the same fate.

Two weeks later, the club sponsored a tournament, and I entered as a bantamweight.

I won.

My father didn't earn enough money for me to join a swanky club like the Nerou Rastey. Membership ran about 30 cents a month, which in those days, for us anyway, was a lot of money. So it was a good thing that the new shah, Mohammad Reza Shah Pahlavi, was such a sports fanatic. He made a point of funding athletic clubs in Iran, including the Nerou Rastey — and, by extension, me. As a result, I was permitted to continue training at the club. After a time, I was even invited to the shah's palace to watch an exhibition match with the king's sisters and daughter. We all got tea and two cookies, the first cookies I'd ever eaten in my life. They were so good, I can taste them still.

At the time, boxing as a sport was relatively new in Iran. It really didn't catch on there until World War II, when foreign officers and soldiers indulged in the occasional bout. As such, only a few of the trainers at the club actually had experience in the ring; the others went by what they saw in the movies. Learning to box from them was like trying to learn English from someone who'd never heard the language spoken.

Fortunately, though, I'd seen a fair amount of boxing at the camp where all the American, British, and Russian soldiers lived during the war. I watched those bouts with a keen eye, noticing the way the boxers stood, the way they moved their feet, the way they timed their punches, and incorporated much of what I saw into my own fighting style. Once, I even saw Joe Louis take the ring. He shadowboxed some American soldiers. They didn't hit each other, but it was nevertheless fun to watch. After he was finished, Joe climbed out of the ring and walked toward the big hall where some entertainers were singing. I was little, so I was able to squeak my way through the crowd to reach him. I said "Hello!" He smiled, shook hands with me, put his hand on my head, and walked away.

(Watching boxing is still one of my favorite things to do, especially from the comfort of my own home. I get 700 channels on my satellite dish, so it seems like there's always a match going on. I especially like Roy Jones, Jr., Oscar de la Hoya, and Evander Holyfield because in addition to being good fighters, they're decent people. So many boxers only know how to fight. That's okay inside the ring, but outside, you have to be a nice human being. You have to have some class.)

Eventually, I caught the attention of Hans Ziglarski, a trainer at the Nerou Rastey who *did* know his stuff. Ziglarski had represented Germany as a bantamweight in the 1932 Olympics in Los Angeles, claiming the silver medal after losing a hard-fought bout with Horace "Lefty" Gwynne.

Ziglarski taught me two things: One, always shave your

armpits. That way, even if you only took one bath a week, like I did, you wouldn't smell like a zoo. It itched like hell at first, but I got used to it after a while, and still do it today. Two, you don't win a fight in the ring; you win it during the months beforehand. If you enter the ring healthy and prepared, you'll be hard to beat.

After months of preparation under Ziglarski's watchful eye, and with my underarms suitably bald, I entered the ring at the Tehran City Championships as a bantamweight, and I won. Next, I entered the Iranian national tournament, again as a bantamweight, and won that too; my prize was a medal — it was real 24-carat gold, you could bend it — given to me by the shah himself. Finally, I was invited to an Olympic trial, where I again dominated my weight class, thereby earning the right to join the 1948 Iranian Olympic squad.

I was 17.

The 1948 Olympiad was particularly special for two reasons. One, it was the first time that Iran had ever competed in the Olympic Games. Two, it was the first time that the Games had been held since 1936, the year Adolph Hitler played host in Berlin. (Hitler's attempts to hijack that Olympiad to showcase the so-called "superiority" of Aryan athletes were thwarted by the heroics of the African-American sprinter, Jesse Owens.) Japan, slated to host the 1940 games, withdrew its bid in 1938; officials blamed ongoing clashes with neighboring China for the decision. Desperate, the International Olympic Committee scrambled to transfer the Olympiad to Helsinki, Finland, but the advent of World War II — specifically, the Soviet Union's invasion of Finland and Hitler's march on Poland in 1939 — squashed that idea. And of course, the cancellation of the 1944 Games due to the war was predictable. By then, that Olympiad's designated host, London, was under constant attack by Hitler's Luftwaffe.

As a symbolic gesture following the Allied victory in 1945, the International Olympic Committee tapped London to host the 1948 Games even though much of the city had been bombed to rubble during the war. In another symbolic gesture, the IOC snubbed Axis powers Germany and Japan; athletes representing those nations were not permitted to participate. The Soviet Union, though invited, declined to attend.

As for me, I received a snubbing of my own — by the Iranian Olympic Committee. Incredibly, even though I had clearly qualified for the Iranian team, I was told by committee officials that I would not attend the 1948 Olympiad. "You're too young," they said. "You don't have enough experience." To be fair, I was only 17, and I had only a year of boxing under my belt, but I had beaten everyone they could throw at me. And besides, how would I ever gain experience if I wasn't given the opportunity to compete? I argued my case, but my efforts were in vain. The decision had been made.

So I hatched a plan.

First, I penned a letter to the shah, pleading my case. I don't remember its exact words, but in effect, it noted that although I'd qualified for the Iranian Olympic squad, I'd been barred from attending the Games. I acknowledged that I might not win a medal, but stated that the experience of competing in London would almost certainly enable me to improve, to better represent Iran in future events. I asked him if he would consider overruling the committee's decision.

Next, I asked an acquaintance of mine named Aftondelian to deliver the letter for me. In those days, Aftondelian was the top tennis player in Iran, and was frequently summoned to hit around with the shah. He graciously agreed, and invited me to join him the next time he was invited to play at the shah's palace.

A few days later, with the letter safely in my breast pocket, I clambered aboard the Jeep that had been sent to ferry us to the palace. When we arrived, Aftondelian slipped the letter onto the shah's chair; as the shah zinged winner after winner past Aftondelian, who had wisely opted to throw the game, I waited, breathless, for him to open it. Finally, after what seemed like an eternity of play, the exhausted shah plucked the letter from his seat, sat down, read it, looked at me, and nodded.

The next day, I was invited to the Olympic training camp.

On the morning of our scheduled departure for London, the government sent a bus around to convey all the athletes on the Iranian squad and their families to Tehran's Mehrabad Airport. When it came for me, I lugged my bag — which was stuffed to the gills with clothes and food for a family friend who was attending school in London — onto the bus with my mother, my father, and my brother Issar in tow. When we arrived at the airport, 6,000 people greeted us, shouting and cheering, to wish us luck.

After kissing my mother goodbye and shaking my father's and brother's hands, I crossed the tarmac, ascended the Jetway stairs, and boarded the London-bound propeller plane. With a pair of seats on each side of the center aisle, about a dozen rows in all, the plane's cabin had plenty of room for the entire team — roughly 35 athletes — and our coaches. We were palpably excited, as evidenced by our constant chatter, by our easy laughter. Any natural shyness we might have felt toward our fellow athletes had been extinguished during training camp. Besides, most of us knew each other from competitions at various clubs around town.

I staked out a window seat and, as we hopped from Tehran to Cairo, I watched, fascinated, as the sea swallowed the pimpled brown land beneath me. It was a smooth flight. I know that several people were terrified of flying, but I was not. I was thrilled. This was my first time on an airplane — hell, my first time leaving Tehran, period — and I intended to savor every moment.

After fueling up in Cairo we skipped to Rome, where we stayed in a nice hotel overnight. Somehow, a few of the guys managed to misplace their passports, despite the fact we never left the hotel. They were afraid they'd be denied entry into England, but some quick footwork by the Iranian embassy ironed things out for them.

Finally, nearly a day after we'd left Tehran, we touched down in London, where I was immediately struck by the sheer number of planes at the airport. Unlike Mehrabad Airport in Tehran, where two or three planes arrived and departed each week, London's Heathrow Airport was teeming with aircraft both on the ground and in the sky. I watched planes bearing athletes from all over the world — the Olympic rings had been painted onto the planes' tails — circle and land. I saw the shah's private plane touch down.

After retrieving our luggage and clearing customs, we piled into a double-decker bus and made for our lodgings, which were situated close to Wembley Stadium. As the bus hurtled across London, an Englishman spoke to us in Persian about British etiquette, cautioning us not to spit or litter on the street.

As he lectured, I pressed my face against the window and watched the city blur by. London swarmed with people, and for me, everything was new: the architecture; the weather; the (relatively) ordered traffic; the pale populace; the bright lights; the food; the noise.

Although the war had been over for three years, there were soldiers everywhere. Rubble and wreckage remained where grand structures once stood, evidence of the Blitz's toll. Even as late as 1948, Britain continued to be in the throes of a post-war depression; indeed, bread rationing remained in effect until the very day the Olympic Games began. It was not in the budget to build new facilities for the events; instead, old standbys like Wembley Stadium and the adjoining Empire Pool were tapped as venues. Likewise, the construction of an Olympic Village was out of the question, causing officials to stow athletes in colleges and in barracks around the city. My accommodations were in one of countless two-storey longhouses that had been built during the war to house American troops. In fact, my quarters there weren't unlike the ones I enjoyed at home: 10 of us, all boxers, in a single room.

The Opening Ceremonies at Wembley Stadium were an event to remember. They were held on July 29, 1948, a Thursday; if memory serves, that day was the *only* day during the London Olympiad that it didn't rain. The athletes, more than 4,000 in all, gathered in the stadium. Entering in alphabetical order by country, participants from India and Iraq sandwiched our contingent. Unlike most of the other athletes, who wore ordinary suits, we looked like policemen in our navy-blue collared uniforms and white hats, but we were comfortable. All around us, athletes took photographs with their own cameras, but of course, I didn't have one, nor did any other members of the Iranian squad. A camera was a luxury, like a watch. (We'd brought a team photographer, but you had to kiss his butt to get him to take a picture.) When the sea of athletes crested in front of King George, we stopped, and turned to face him. After a trumpet fanfare and a 21-gun salute, the Olympic flag was raised, the Olympic flame was lit, and the organizers released thousands of pigeons — one for every athlete in the Games — into the sky.

They'd been caged so long, half the pigeons fell mid-flight.

Afterward, two members of each country's team were invited to tea at Buckingham Palace, and because I was the youngest member of the Iranian group, I was chosen to attend along with our team's wrestler, who was selected for his considerable talent. Chaperoned by an Iranian general, the wrestler and I were admitted into the palace. We drank some English tea and ate some crumbly cookies. Before that, I'd only tasted those two cookies at the shah's palace; sweets at home were limited to raisins, dates, things like that. I went a little crazy even though I was due to weigh in the next day — fortunately, I didn't blow my weight class. Later, we shook hands with the King and Queen of England. King George spoke to me, but I didn't speak English, so I could only nod dumbly before being escorted away.

As a participating athlete, I was allowed into any event I wanted to watch, and could use the buses and subways for free. So in the days leading up to my bouts, I watched a lot of soccer, swimming, wrestling, and track and field, which, in those days, occurred at the beginning of the Games instead of at the end. I felt terribly proud watching one of my Iranian teammates — a skinny guy who fidgeted endlessly — complete the marathon. He was nowhere near

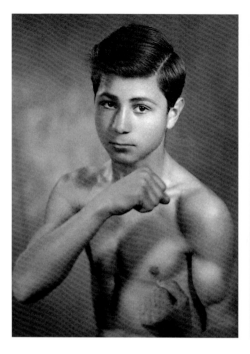

Mike Agassi, crowned Bantamweight
Champion, Tehran, Iran, 1948

Mike, American Mission Church, Tehran,
Iran, 1949

Mike in the ring at
the Nerou Rastey
club, Tehran, 1949

Mike far left with boxing friends Benny, David, and Lucy, 1950

Mike (sixth from right), Egypt, 1950

Mike outside the gym in Tehran during boxing practice, 1951

Friends and teachers on last day of school, 1951

Mike shakes hands with the shah of Iran, King's Palace, 1952

Mike with his boxing coach,
Hans Ziglarski, Helsinki, 1952

Mike at the Olympic Games with Bantam boxer Nick Khah, Helsinki, 1952

Mike's parents, Noonia and David Agassi,
Tehran, Iran, 1952

Mike with his mother and his
cousin Joseph

Mike and Betty's wedding, Ivanhoe Restaurant, Chicago, 1959

Newlyweds Betty and Mike with Mike's sister, Helen, Chicago, 1960

Mike and Sam Agassi, Chicago, 1961

Mike, Rita, and Betty, Chicago, 1961

Sam with Rita, 1961

Mike by the house on Tara Street,
Las Vegas

Betty, Rita, and Phillip, Las Vegas, 1963

Rita, Betty, and Phillip, Las Vegas, 1964

Phillip on court with Mike, Las Vegas, 1966

Mike gives Phillip and Rita a tennis lesson, 1966

Mike's mother with Tami Agassi, Las Vegas, 1969

Mike, John Wojcik, Phillip, Rita, Mariann Wojcik, John Jr., Mrs. Wojcik,
Landmark Hotel, 1970

Rita and Phillip, Tropicana Hotel tennis courts, Las Vegas, 1971

Andre, Rita, and Phillip, Las Vegas, 1974

Rita, Redland tournament winner, California, 1974

the medalists, but he finished nonetheless, which, in my mind, was a gargantuan feat in itself. Packing the highlight reel, though, were the exploits of a 30-year-old Dutch mother of two, Fanny Blankers-Koen, who won the Grand Slam of sprinters, taking gold in the 100-meter dash, the 200-meter dash, the 80-meter hurdles, and, as the anchor, the 4-by-100-meter relay.

Finally, it was my turn to compete. During the 1948 Games, the Empire Pool (later renamed Wembley Arena), in addition to hosting the swimming events, functioned as the boxing venue. Inside the cavernous arena, organizers had built six rings, and I was nervous stepping into the one where my first bout would take place. At 6′2″, give or take an inch, my first opponent, a Spaniard, towered over me. He had long arms, which worked against me, but I figured his physique — he was skinny as a rail — made him vulnerable. After landing several strong punches during the match, I returned to my corner, where my jubilant coach yelled "You won! You won!" The judges, however, thought otherwise. (The next year, that Spaniard won the European Championship as a welterweight.) My second and final match, this one against a South African, ended the same way.

It might sound like sour grapes on my part, but I felt that the judges' biases factored into their decisions far more than my performance had. It just seemed like politics, not boxing, decided my fate. All it takes is a few judges who don't like Iranians, or who do like Spaniards or South Africans, or who just prefer one athlete over another for reasons unknown. That's the way it is anytime you involve judges in a sport. Just look at what happened to Roy Jones, Jr. in the light-middleweight gold-medal match of the 1988 Seoul Games. Even though he beat the snot out of his opponent, South

Korean fighter Si-Hun Park, Jones *still* lost the decision. In that particular case, a subsequent investigation revealed that some of the judges had accepted bribes from Korean officials. No such luck in my case, though.

Ousted early, I had some time to kill, so I decided to check out the All England Lawn Tennis & Croquet Club, where tennis pros play Wimbledon. At first, I thought Wembley Stadium was where Wimbledon was played; the two words sounded so much alike. But after arriving in London I was quickly set straight. I'd heard of Wimbledon, which was then an amateur event and would remain so until 1968, from the British soldiers I'd met at the mission, and had even watched a former Wimbledon champion — his name now escapes me — play an exhibition match at the base in Tehran. Back in Tehran, as I practiced my strokes against the wall at the American Mission Church, I used to pretend I was playing in the Wimbledon finals. Sometimes my opponent was Fred Perry, other times it was Don Budge. But always, *always*, I won the fantasy match.

I asked one of the girls who had been hanging around the stadium the previous few days — athletes had groupies, even then — how to get there. Her name was Adrienne Perry, and her father graciously agreed to drive me. In those days, the club wasn't like it is now. Now, they guard it like it's Fort Knox. Back then, though, they let us in to look around. They gave us a hard time at first, but then they saw my Olympic uniform and opened the doors. The famous grass court was a lovely green, but was devoid of players; indeed, even the net had been taken down. I spied the King and Queen's box. During the war, one well-placed German bomb had struck center court. More than a thousand seats had been demolished, but by 1948, no effects of the bombing lingered. Surrounding the court were thousands of seats, though not so many as there are now, of course. I noticed the calm, the quiet, and imagined how the atmosphere would be changed, charged, during a match.

I knew that I'd never play at Wimbledon. I might someday develop into a decent player, but I'd never compete internationally. My social position, my family's financial situation, had denied me my shot at tennis greatness. But as I pondered that hallowed court on that summer afternoon, I dreamt that someday, somehow, somebody from my family would win this tournament.

Forty-four years later, in 1992, my son Andre did just that.

CHAPTER THREE

"America lives in the heart of every man everywhere who wishes to find a
region where he will be free to work out his destiny as he chooses."
— Woodrow Wilson

Although as a group, the Iranian Olympic athletes hadn't been
terribly successful at the London Olympiad — only one
member, weightlifter Jafar Salmasi, had snagged a medal, a
bronze — we were greeted like kings upon our return, even by the
king himself. We were invited to tea parties at the palace, and the
shah sent us presents on our birthdays. We were in the papers. We
were *somebody*. Strangers stopped us on the street to shake our
hands.

For a kid who'd grown up poor, an outsider, a nobody, it felt
good.

Which is why, although I preferred tennis, I dedicated myself to
boxing. I still hit a tennis ball around whenever I could, but even at
17 I was smart enough to realize that boxing, not tennis, was my
future — for the short term at least. So in the years following the
1948 Games, when I wasn't at school at the American Mission
Church or at home with my parents and siblings, I spent the bulk
of my time in the ring both at the Nerou Rastey club and in

matches abroad — in Egypt, Italy, and Turkey — with an eye toward the 1952 Olympiad in Helsinki.

As before, I won the Tehran City Championships in 1952 — this time as a featherweight — and the National Championships after that. And once again, I qualified for the Olympics.

This time, nobody questioned my right to go.

The 1952 Helsinki Olympiad was far and away more organized than the 1948 Games in London had been. Unlike Great Britain, which had been unable to construct new facilities or housing prior to the event, Finland built state-of-the-art venues for the occasion. And unlike in London, where athletes were housed wherever there was available lodging, competitors in Helsinki — some 5,000 athletes from 69 countries, including former pariah nations like Japan and Germany — enjoyed lodging at a spectacular new Olympic Village. The Soviet Union, attending its first Olympiad since the fall of the czar, insisted on its own separate village, a request begrudgingly granted by the Finns.

As it turned out, the 1952 Games proved much more fruitful for the Iranians than the 1948 Games had been. We claimed seven medals in all — two silvers and three bronzes in freestyle wrestling, and one silver and one bronze in weightlifting. As for me, my bouts went about the same way they had in London: Twice I thought I beat the hell out of my opponent, and twice the judges disagreed.

So be it. It gave me more time to watch my fellow athletes. I caught some track and field and some soccer. I watched American super-heavyweight Ed Sanders slug it out with Ingemar Johansson, a Swede, for the gold. Actually, "slug it out" is a bit of a misnomer. In reality, the Swede, freaked out by Sanders' size and abilities, practically cowered anytime Ed came close. In fact, Johansson's strategy was to stay as far away as possible during the match, prompting officials to disqualify him for "not fighting his best."

Sadly, Ed died in the autumn of 1952 after a blow to the head during a bout with Willy James. Seven years later, Johansson ko'ed Floyd Patterson to win the world heavyweight title. Given Sanders's utter dominance over Johansson at the 1952 Games, you have to wonder what kind of future the guy might have had in the ring.

The highlight of the Helsinki Games for me, though, was shaking hands with German boxing legend Max Schmeling. Schmeling was most famous for stunning Joe Louis as a 10–1 underdog in 1936, knocking him down in the fourth round and knocking him out in the 12th. (Despite their racial differences, Schmeling and Louis, an "Aryan" and a black man, would go on to become lifelong friends. Indeed, Schmeling would serve as pall-bearer at Louis's funeral.) When Hitler used Schmeling's accomplishments in the ring as evidence of Aryan superiority, Schmeling himself was unfairly villainized worldwide; in truth, Schmeling defied Hitler by refusing to join the Nazi Party or to publicize the party line, declining to fire his American Jewish man-ager, and continuing to associate with German Jews. To retaliate, Hitler drafted Schmeling into the Paratroops during World War II in an attempt to send the boxer to his death. After each suicide mis-sion, to Hitler's great consternation, Schmeling sauntered back alive. Years later, Henri Lewin, a German Jew who eventually became a prominent Las Vegas hotelier, credited Schmeling with saving his life and his brother's by stowing them in his Berlin apartment during the pogroms on Kristallnacht and later helping them flee the country — further evidence of Schmeling's anti-Nazi leanings.

The more I traveled, the more I noticed the indignities of life in Iran. There were my family's living arrangements, for one — the lot of us crammed into one dirt-floored room. That's tough to take after experiencing a good night's sleep in an elegant hotel. Even more torturous was queuing up with my neighbors to use facilities that consisted of a fetid hole in the ground after having enjoyed the pleasures of a proper Western toilet. Then there was the fact that my father, nearing 70 years of age, worked himself half to death for a pittance — that is, if he got paid at all. Even the perks I got from being an athlete — those palace tea parties, those nods in the newspaper — weren't enough. I knew my stint as a boxer wouldn't last forever. At some point, I'd be too old to fight, would have to retire. Then what?

It didn't help that in 1951, in defiance of the shah's wishes, Premier Mohammed Mossadeq forced the Majlis to nationalize Iran's British-owned oil industry — a move that prompted Great Britain to impose economic sanctions whose primary effect was to make life harder for people like us. Politically speaking, things got a bit touchy after that. Mossadeq, who was ousted in 1952, returned with a vengeance, gathering enough power to persuade Mohammad Reza Shah to flee that same year. With the support of the CIA, the shah would return in 1953 and overthrow Mossadeq, but things in Iran weren't exactly stable in the interim.

So I set my sights on America.

No doubt my warm feelings toward America stemmed in part from the kindness shown by the G.I.s stationed in Tehran during the war, but the truth is, everyone I knew in Iran wanted to go to the United States. We understood that in America, anybody could be rich. You could have a car. You could have a house. You could have a wife. It was a place where no matter who you were, no matter where you came from, you could be a success — provided you worked hard.

Leaving Iran posed a couple of obstacles. First, all able-bodied Iranian males age 20 and up were required by law to serve two years in the Iranian Army; needless to say, as a 21-year-old two-time Olympian, I was considered "able-bodied." Second, Iranian males who had not served in the army were not permitted to obtain a passport — *except* in special circumstances, like, say, having competed abroad in the 1948 and 1952 Olympic Games. Unfortunately, however, I'd been forced to surrender my passport upon returning from the Helsinki Games, after which it was locked away in a government office located in a sports arena where it was meant to remain until I fulfilled my conscription obligation.

But I had a secret: Before surrendering my passport, I had colored the bottom corner of it with a black marker — just a tick, enough to identify it in a stack as mine. And one day, I just so happened to be in the office where my passport was stored, and just so happened to notice it in a pile, and *just so happened* to pocket it when no one was around.

Passport in hand, I wrote my brother Samuel, who, having fulfilled his conscription obligation, had immigrated to America in 1950 and was living in Chicago. He was making good money working as a waiter at the Conrad Hilton, and sent me funds to buy a plane ticket to New York; I'd take a bus the rest of the way once I arrived.

Normally, when you bought a plane ticket, you showed the

ticket agent your passport; the agent would then contact the Iranian government to ensure that you were eligible to leave the country — which would certainly blow my cover. So when I bought my ticket at eight o'clock on a November morning in 1952 for a flight at 4:00 p.m. that afternoon, I promised the agent I'd bring him my passport later that day, but conveniently "forgot" to do so. Instead, ticket in hand, I went home, gathered my things, and made for the airport.

Before I left, I said goodbye to my family. That was difficult. I was happy to be going to the United States, but I knew I was never coming back. I suspected I might see my mother, my brothers, and my sister again — I guessed they might follow Sam and me to America — but I knew it was the last time I'd see my dad. He was an old man by then, nearly 70.

"Don't forget us," my father said. "Don't forget us." He pressed his Bible into my hands. He never kissed us, but he kissed me then. My mother was more demonstrative, weeping, kissing my legs, my knees, my face.

Indeed, just as I'd predicted, that was the last time I saw my father. He died of old age 10 years later, in 1962, and was buried at the Armenian cemetery in Tehran. Thinking about it breaks my heart even now.

At the airport, when it was time to board the plane, two government agents manned the gate to scrutinize each passenger's passport. My heart pounding in my chest, I sandwiched myself in the queue. I was terrified. What if they discovered what I'd done? Would I go to jail? Or worse? But I had to go through with it. Come what may, I had to at least take a shot at leaving.

"Passport," demanded one of the agents.

With a gulp, I handed it over, and held my breath as the man flipped it open.

"Emmanuel Agassi," he said, an eyebrow cocked. I nodded glumly. Christ, I was done. They were going to cuff me and drag me off. I just knew it.

But then, incredibly, a wide grin spread across the agent's face. "The boxer!" he exclaimed. "From the Olympics!"

"Yes!" I said, smiling back. "That's right!"

"Emmanuel Agassi, the boxer!" the agent called to his colleague, pointing at me.

"From the Olympics!" his colleague called back.

Good God, I thought. This just might work. I figured I should cement the deal, though.

"You know," I said, casually pulling a wad of Persian currency — the equivalent of about $10 in American money — from my pocket. "I cannot use this where I'm going. Would you like it?"

The agent gratefully accepted my offer, gave my passport a cursory glance, and sent me on my way.

Outside, I ascended the stairs to the plane, found my seat, and sat quietly, perfectly still. *Breathe*, I thought. *Act natural.* I stayed that way, terrified, until the plane took off; only after we were airborne did I finally relax.

Like my parents before me, I had left the country of my birth.

And like them, I would never return.

I was too keyed up to sleep on the flight out of Tehran, so by the time we touched down in Paris, I was exhausted. After disembarking, I carefully placed my things behind my chair in the terminal and caught a quick nap. I had wisely kept my luggage to a minimum: a few belongings in a suitcase, my passport, my medical history (including chest X-rays, a head X-ray, and the results of various blood and urine tests, all culled for the Helsinki Olympics), and, less wisely, a 10-pound bag of rice I had foolishly agreed to deliver to the son of a neighbor. My careful packing, however, meant nothing in the end; awakened abruptly from a deep sleep by calls for my next flight, I panicked and bolted for the gate, leaving my papers — passport, medical history, everything — behind. I did not realize my mistake until hours later. High above the Atlantic, I burst into the plane's cockpit — this was before cockpit doors were more securely padlocked than a safe-deposit box in a Swiss bank — and begged the pilots to turn back, to no avail of course. Sensitive to my plight, however, the pilots did manage to track down my papers via radio, and assured me they'd arrive on the next flight.

As promised, my things did arrive, but by then I'd been carted off to Ellis Island where I would remain, inexplicably, for two and a half weeks. I was treated well, given a bed in a room that slept 10 (like being back home!), fed three square meals a day. But it was scary, too, because every person around me — the other inmates, the people in charge — was from a different place and spoke a different language. And even though my passport and medical records arrived early in my stay, U.S. officials demanded that I be re-examined to ensure I hadn't contracted any diseases from my fellow immigrants during my time at Ellis Island. Just as I had been before the Helsinki Games, I was again subjected to blood tests, urine tests, a chest X-ray, and a head X-ray. Which was fine, really, except that the officials confused my results with those of another guy with a similar name, and denied me entry because I had, they thought, a heart murmur. I have never been so happy as when, two days later, they told me they were mistaken.

Finally, after 17 days of waiting, I was granted entry into the country. They put me on a boat to Manhattan, where a taxi was waiting for me.

"Where to?" said the cabbie.

"Chicago," I replied.

After some confusion, we established that I did not, in fact, want to take a cab to Chicago; rather, I wanted to go to the bus station, where I could catch the next Greyhound to the Windy City.

"Why not take a train?" he asked.

I said, as best I could with my minimal English, "With a bus, I can see more."

After paying for the cab, forking over some cash to call my brother in Chicago to tell him I was coming, and spending $22 on my bus ticket, I began my journey.

I had $4 in my pocket.

In contrast to the bustle of New York, which looked like the America I'd seen in my mind's eye all those years, I was shocked by the empty land that enveloped the highway outside of town. America wasn't so different from Iran in that way. I was disheartened to discover, too, that the bus route tended to bypass the larger cities en route. The bus was virtually empty, so I gazed out the window in silence, watching fields and woods stream past. I learned a few English words on the way, among them "limit," as in "city limit."

Every so often, the bus would stop at restaurants. The driver would say, "You have 20 minutes!" But I had no watch. And I didn't have much money anyway, so instead of sitting down for a proper meal, I just ate candy. During the whole 28-hour bus ride, I lived on chocolate candy, which I bought from vending machines, five bars for a quarter.

Finally, an eternity after leaving Tehran, I arrived in Chicago on December 7, 1952. As the bus groaned toward the station, I soaked in the city's lights, its towering buildings and cavernous streets. My brother Sam was waiting for me outside the terminal alongside his brand-new, blue, two-door 1952 Ford — living proof of the bounty that was America. We drove to the YMCA he called home, and, after paying to park his car — I remember being shocked by that — we went inside and plunked down $14 to rent a room for me for a week.

"Name?" asked the clerk.

Names are so important; they have so much to do with an individual's personality, with what kind of person he or she becomes. Take the name Phil. Have you ever met a Phil who wasn't easygoing? My oldest son is named Phil, Phillip, and that's just what he is: Easygoing. Or consider the name Andre. It's an aggressive name, a flamboyant name, and that's just how my son Andre turned out to be.

So I thought a moment, and answered "Mike Agassi." Mike was a simple name and I liked it. It sounded American. Honorable. More importantly, it was a name I could spell.

Before long, I enrolled in a high-school English course at the YMCA and got a job at the Conrad Hilton as an elevator operator. I started in the service elevator, but because I was always neat and clean — shaved, clean cut, just as my old boxing coach, Hans Ziglarski, had taught me — I was quickly promoted to the public elevator. After being shocked by requests from male guests to procure women for their entertainment, however, I requested a transfer back to the service elevator, and management complied. I also found an apartment on Huron Street, close to my job. It was a one-bedroom affair that I shared with a few other working types. Compared to what I was used to in Iran, it was heaven; then again, I would have said that about any living arrangements that included a proper toilet.

Because I knew I would need course credits to renew my visa, I applied to Roosevelt University, where my brother was studying. (Fortunately for him, he married an American woman not long after I arrived in Chicago, which meant he was eligible to receive a green card.) Although the university rejected my application — I failed the standardized test because I hadn't learned much English yet — I was permitted to study as a student at large, so I enrolled. At first, the only class I could take was math because it didn't require a strong grasp of English (although I had attended school at the American Mission Church in Tehran, my courses had been taught in Persian) and because I had already covered a lot of the material back home. That helped me to be a fairly good student. Eventually, the university admitted me as a full-fledged enrollee — I majored in mathematics and minored in physics — and I completed my bachelor's degree in 1959.

In those early months, my inability to speak or understand English made life quite difficult. What was especially problematic was grasping slang. Someone would say "How's it going?" and I would wonder, what is going? Where? Worse, a lot of words in

English sound the same but mean different things. Those really threw me off. Fortunately, though, Persian is distantly related to English, and some words sound similar. For example, the Persian word for "brother" is "beradar"; "father" is "pedar"; and "mother" is "mader." Slowly, I began to absorb the language, but it did take a while.

There were a few instances when my skills as a boxer came in handy. The first was the day after I arrived in Chicago, when some gentlemen at the YMCA got, shall we say, overly friendly in the communal shower. I was shy, and preferred to bathe in my briefs; when some guys tried to embarrass me — and God knows what else — by pulling my briefs down, I knocked one of them out cold. It was quite an event. The police came, and my brother had to explain what had happened. In any case, I was left alone in the shower after that.

Another time, after I'd begun taking an engineering course at Roosevelt University, I was carefully treading across the slushy sidewalk to avoid stepping in a puddle and ruining my shoes, carrying a gigantic portfolio filled with engineering drawings I'd completed as a homework assignment. Suddenly, some guy bumped me, hard, and I fell, my drawings flying everywhere. When I looked up to see who had hit me, there were three guys standing over me, just like in the movies. As I scrambled to my feet, one of them came forward and barked at me in English. I didn't understand exactly what he said, but I did understand that he was looking for trouble. I stayed cool, trying to figure out what he was going to do, keeping one eye on his hands and another on the two guys behind him. He drew his right hand back, about to swing, and I punched him — a right jab — and knocked him out. A second guy came at me, and I flattened him as well. The third guy took off running.

As I gathered my wits — not to mention my drawings — a couple of policemen came along. They tried to talk to me, but I didn't understand English well enough by then to follow. They could tell by my clothes and by my portfolio that I wasn't some bum on the street looking for trouble, so they brought all three of us — me and the two guys I'd flattened — to the station, and fetched an interpreter from the Iranian embassy to mediate our discussion. All three of us filed complaints, and although we were scheduled to see a judge in 30 days, we settled out of court. I was relieved that the whole ordeal was over, but was more determined than ever to improve my grasp of English.

In addition to prompting me to cultivate my language skills, these experiences also served as a powerful reminder of my abilities as a fighter. Before long, I began exploring Chicago's boxing scene. One day, a cousin of mine on my father's side, Sam Ohannes, took me to his Catholic Youth Organization (CYO) club — a free boxing gym about a block away from Roosevelt University — and introduced me around. The gym had lots of equipment — gloves, a ring, some bags.

Right away, I changed into my workout clothes, took their bag gloves, which were different from regular punching gloves, and started hitting on a bag. Within minutes, a cluster of trainers had gathered around me. They saw I had speed, I had punch.

I returned the next day, and again, the trainers put me on a bag. This time, though, there was a new guy amongst the coaches: Tony Zale. Zale was, without question, among the dominant middleweights of his era. Nicknamed "The Man of Steel," he'd turned pro in 1934 after working the steel mills in his hometown of Gary, Indiana, and had quickly gained a reputation for being impervious to pain. Just when you thought he was done for, down for the count, he'd crawl back up and whale away at his opponent like no tomorrow. He had an unbelievable punch; one opponent described being hit by Zale as feeling like "someone stuck a red-hot poker in you and left it there."

Zale claimed the National Boxing Association Middleweight title in 1940 and successfully defended it three times before enlisting with the U.S. Navy after the bombing of Pearl Harbor. There's a famous story about Zale's arrival at boot camp: When he got there, Zale told the registration officer his legal name, Anthony Zaleski, and his occupation, professional middleweight boxer. The officer replied, "I'd hate to be in your shoes, Zaleski. Tony Zale's due in here this week." After the war, Zale returned to the ring. And although he quickly ticked off several wins, many thought his best years were a casualty of the war — until 1946, when Zale met a slugger from Manhattan's Lower East Side named Rocky Graziano in the ring at Yankee Stadium.

In front of 40,000 screaming fans, Zale, the underdog, landed a classic left hook in round one, dropping Graziano for a four count. Graziano charged back in the second, windmilling, flailing, landing a flurry of punches, splitting Zale's lip. In the third, Graziano's fury continued. He pounded Zale into the canvas, but Zale teetered to his feet after a count of three; his handlers dragged him to his corner at the end of the round. After five, Zale was all but finished as fans called for an end to the fight, but incredibly, inexplicably, he was reborn in the sixth. He felled Graziano with a deadly right to the ribs. Graziano staggered to his feet, only to be dropped again by a perfect left hook to the chin.

That time, Graziano did not get up.

Zale, at 33 years of age, after a bout that *Ring Magazine* would later call the fourth greatest fight of all time, had reclaimed the World Middleweight title. It was the beginning of a great rivalry, which would bring a rematch in Chicago in 1947, equally as vicious as the first, but won by Graziano. A rubber match in 1948 in Newark, arguably the most brutal of all, would return the belt to Zale. Three months later, however, Zale would surrender the title to the European Middleweight champ, Frenchman Marcel Cerdan, in a 12-round TKO.

After that, Zale hung up his gloves for good and signed on as the head boxing coach at the Chicago CYO, which was how he wound up watching me work out on the bag in early 1953. I'd heard of him, of course, and recognized him straight away, but I wasn't particularly star-struck. By then, I'd seen enough boxing greats — Louis, Schmeling, Sanders — to keep my head. As for Zale, if I may say so, he fell in love with me immediately (in a manner of speaking). He said he'd never seen such quick hands, such punches. His only gripe was that I didn't try to hit that hard *all* the time. In any case, he put me in an exhibition match the next day.

For me, it was déjà vu all over again. I beat the hell out of the guy, but the decision went against me anyway. I went to the judges and said, "What fight were you watching? Look at my face! Look at his face! Whose is bloodier?"

But Tony Zale told me, "You beat him. Don't worry about it."

So I didn't.

With Tony's help, I began training for the Chicago Golden

Gloves tournament, which I won as a featherweight in 1953, just four months after arriving in America.

Soon after, I was approached by a boxing manager and promoter named Sam about going pro. Sam was a chiseler, chipping small sums from each of the 10 or 12 boxers — hacks, mostly — that he managed, taking $15 here, $20 there. One day he handed me a piece of paper. "Sign this," he said. "I'll get you some fights and make you some money."

I said, "I don't know. I'll fight, and I'll pay you whether I win or lose, but I don't want to sign anything."

Sam reluctantly agreed to my terms, and as promised, got me a fight — at Madison Square Garden in New York. My match was to be against a relative novice who had only seven or eight fights under his belt, and would precede the main event: Randy Turpin, the tattooed Brit (who was, incidentally, deaf — it just goes to show you what you can overcome if you put your mind to it), and Carl "Bobo" Olson, who hailed from Hawaii, battling for the World Middleweight title in front of some 18,000 spectators. My take was to be $88.

I ran the numbers. A train from Chicago to New York and back would cost $44. I could expect to pay $6 a day for a room and $5 a day for food. On top of that, I'd have to give my manager $20. Depending on how long I stayed in Manhattan, there was a good chance I wouldn't break even. Then again, I thought, it *was* a way to get a foot in the door. Maybe future bouts would be more profitable. So I agreed to participate.

On the day of the fight, a doctor examined my opponent and me. He weighed us, took our temperature, examined our eyes, nose, and ears, told us to turn our heads and cough. Long story short, I passed, the other guy didn't. I'm not sure why. I think he had a cold or something. I was philosophical about it; I figured, at least I'd get to watch the championship fight. But an hour later, my manager told me he'd found another guy for me to fight — only this guy was no novice. He had fought dozens of times. And although they didn't weigh him, he looked like a welterweight to me, and here I was, a featherweight. I swear, he was huge.

This guy was going to beat the shit out of me.

"This is your chance for instant recognition!" my manager urged, shaking my shoulders. I had too much pride to say no, but not enough to actually fight this guy. So I beelined for the locker room, packed my things, hucked my suitcase out a window, crawled out after it, and caught the next train back to Chicago.

Although my professional boxing career ended before it had even begun, I continued to box the amateur circuit, and again won the Golden Gloves Championship in Chicago in 1954 as a featherweight and in 1955 as a lightweight.

After I won that first Golden Gloves competition in 1953, I proudly showed the medal I'd earned to my boss at the Conrad Hilton. I thought he would be happy. Instead, he said, in all seriousness, "Go run your elevator."

I was crushed.

One day, I was unable to make it into work. I can't remember why — maybe I was sick, or my car wouldn't start. In any case, I was an idiot and didn't call in, and they fired me. Fortunately, however, some Armenian friends quickly found me a job at the Ambassador East Hotel as a bus boy in the Pump Room.

In 1954, the Pump Room was one of the best dining rooms in the country. With its famed Booth One, where everyone who was anyone was seated, the Pump Room was *the* place to see and be seen. Luminaries like John Barrymore and Bette Davis ate there. It was where Humphrey Bogart and Lauren Bacall celebrated their nuptials. A young Liza Minelli and her mother, Judy Garland, were also frequent guests. In fact, Judy Garland immortalized the Pump Room by singing "We'll eat at the Pump Room/Ambassador East, to say the least" in the musical *Chicago*.

Working in the Pump Room among the Limoges china and the crystal chandeliers was wonderful. Even better were my bosses. When they found out I had won the Golden Gloves, they were terribly impressed. They started calling me "Champ." Once, I was scheduled to work on the same evening as a fight. My boss said, "Okay, go ahead, fight, and come back afterward," so I did.

"What happened?" he asked when I returned. "Did you win?"

"I knocked him out," I said, smiling.

"Atta boy, Champ."

Later on, anytime I went to fight, half the staff would come to watch.

One of my bouts was televised in the greater Chicago area. It was the final of the cyo national tournament. I knocked my opponent out in 30 seconds, and won the Most Outstanding Fighter trophy. Afterward, the president of the Ambassador East Hotel, Mr. Hart, invited me to his office and gave me $50 as a bonus. That was a lot of money then.

Eventually, I was promoted to waiter, which meant I put a lot more money in my pocket after each shift. As a waiter at the Pump Room, I always felt wealthy. I didn't use a bank, so I carried $1,000, even $2,000 with me all the time. After traveling from New York to Chicago with just $4 in my pocket, it felt comforting to carry that wad of cash! Once, after totaling my 1952 Mercury, I sold it for scrap to the dealer; before the ink on the deal was dry, I walked across the street to a Volkswagen showroom and bought a new car with cash. I nearly totaled that one, too, on the way out of the lot; fortunately, it was just a near miss. I guess I've never been much of a driver.

Since I was earning a good income, I sent money back to Iran to help my family. I thought about them all the time. Although my mom and dad could live on $25 every two or three months, I made sure to send them that amount on a monthly basis so they'd have money for some luxuries. With my help, they bought a piece of land and built a multi-room house.

As far as I was concerned, I had made it.

CHAPTER FOUR

"A man with a virtuous wife will have few troubles."
— Chinese proverb

By 1956 or so, I'd begun to realize that my boxing career would not last forever — a notion that was only strengthened when my brother Sam asked if I was getting punchy. Apparently, I'd been talking to myself a lot without even realizing it. A few too many blows to the head, I guess.

So finally, after years of putting my true passion on the back burner, I shifted my full attention to tennis.

When you think about it, going from boxing to tennis is not such a leap. In fact, the great Bud Collins once called tennis "boxing without blood," and in many ways, he's right. A singles tennis match, like a boxing match, is essentially a slugfest between two athletes. The main difference is that you slug with a racket rather than with your fists, and you hit a ball rather than a body. There are other similarities, too: Both sports rely heavily on foot-work and balance, and on hand-eye coordination. And the same snap of the wrist that intensifies a punch can make a tennis ball rocket off the head of the racket.

As for me, I had good foot speed and quick reflexes that enabled me to hit the ball almost immediately after it bounced, while it was still on the rise. And of course, I hit each ball as hard as I could. That was just my nature, I guess. Even so, I'd say I was a fair player at best. I wasn't terribly accurate, and I didn't have much in the way of shot selection.

What I lacked in skill, though, I made up for in enthusiasm, even saving my money to buy films of tournaments and to rent the projector required to watch them. Anytime the pro tour came through town, whether it stopped at Northwestern University, Fullerton Tennis Club, or Chicago University, I made a point to attend, and sometimes volunteered to work the matches as a line judge. I saw all the greats of the day: Ken Rosewall, Pancho Gonzalez, Jack Kramer, to name a few.

So when, in the late 1950s, the Australian and American Davis Cup teams held a banquet at the Ambassador West, which was right across the street from the Ambassador East, where I usually worked, I was nearly beside myself. The Davis Cup has lost some of its luster in recent years; it just hasn't kept up with the times. But back then it was a big deal, on par with the Grand Slams. That year, Australia overpowered the U.S. 3-2 despite predictions by the American captain, Perry Jones, that the Americans would whitewash the Aussies 5-0.

The Aussies' win was no real surprise; in those days, tennis was huge in Australia, and remains so today. Indeed, the Aussies claimed the Davis Cup an unprecedented 15 times during the 1950s and 1960s. (Their only losses were to the USA, in 1954, 1958, 1963, and 1968.)

Besides, that year, 1959, Australia's Davis Cup team was arguably tantamount to USA Basketball's Dream Team of the 1990s. There was Neale Fraser, who, during the course of his career, would win all four Grand Slams in doubles, and who would later captain Australia's Davis Cup team for a record-breaking 23 years — masterminding four victories along the way. There was the great Roy Emerson, who would become the only male player in history to win singles and doubles titles at all four Grand Slam events. Indeed, Emerson, though overshadowed early in his career by Aussie legends Lew Hoad and Ken Rosewall, would claim 12 Grand Slam titles in all — a record that would remain unbroken for more than 30 years. (Not to diminish Emerson's accomplishments, but it should be noted here that when Emerson won his Grand Slam titles, it was before the Open era, which meant that the best players had all turned pro and were therefore ineligible to play the Slams.) And rounding out the team was the man who, many argued, was the best to ever play the game: Rod Laver. In 1962, he became only the second man to complete a singles Grand Slam — that is, he claimed all four Grand Slam crowns during that calendar year — a feat he would repeat in 1969, after the advent of the Open era.

After working the dining room, I stripped off the red jacket and tails that were part of my uniform and returned to listen in. Later, I shook hands with several players, including Fraser, Laver, and Emerson, and their legendary captain, Harry Hopman. And I didn't pass up my chance to meet Perry Jones, Barry MacKay, Butch Buchholz, and Alex Olmedo of the USA.

"One day," I told them, full of bravado, "somebody in my family is going to win the Davis Cup!"

They probably thought I was crazy. Maybe I was. But I was also right: 30 years later, my son Andre became a Davis Cup champion.

I was 28 in the spring of 1959, just finishing my mathematics degree at Roosevelt University, when a Greek girl named Anastasia cornered me after class one day to find out whether I was planning to attend a dance being held later that summer.

"No," I said. "I don't have a girlfriend." By then, I'd been in Chicago for more than six years, but I'd been busy learning English, boxing, working, attending school, playing tennis, and establishing myself in my adopted country. In other words, I had been too busy for girls. That didn't mean I wasn't interested, of course, but most of the women I met in those early years in Chicago were too fussy, too brazen, too boring, or too easy for my taste.

"No girlfriend?" said Anastasia. "I'll find you one!"

Two weeks later, Anastasia cornered me again. "There's a new girl in town," she said. "She doesn't have a boyfriend yet."

I hesitated.

"Don't waste time!" she said. "Call her. She's pretty, and it won't be long before someone else snaps her up!"

Okay, I thought. It can't hurt to call.

"What's her name?" I asked.

"Betty. Betty Dudley. Here's her number."

I called. She sounded nice on the phone, so I asked her out to coffee, and she agreed.

On the evening of our date, I put on a nice suit and drove my vw to the Girls' Club dormitory where Betty was staying. I parked the car and ambled to the lounge to wait, and I watched what seemed like hundreds of girls enter and leave. I wondered, were these girls Betty's spies? Maybe they were reporting back to her what I looked like. Worse, maybe Betty herself had walked in, taken one look at me, and walked right back out. I might not have been tall, per se, but I was dark, and handsome enough — at least I thought so anyway. But there's no accounting for taste.

Finally, after what seemed like an eternity, Betty entered the lounge. Anastasia had been right: Betty *was* pretty. She had mahogany hair, blue eyes, and pale skin, and she wore a dark straight skirt and an off-white blouse that tied on top. She was also a little shy and, I suspect, a bit nervous. When we introduced ourselves, she barely looked at me. I told her that my vw was parked outside, and she made straight for it. If she had been a cartoon character, she would have left a little dust cloud behind as she hustled for the door.

We didn't talk much at first, but soon, a word escaped her lips here and there. As for me, I just drove. I drove and drove and drove, miles and miles. I'm not sure why, exactly; I suppose I just didn't want to let her go. She probably thought I was a serial killer, heading for a remote spot.

Finally, we stopped at a restaurant, and her shyness dissolved. We ordered some sandwiches, and we talked. And talked. It was so long ago, I barely remember what we talked about; our families, I suppose. I learned that Betty, born in November of 1937, had two sisters: one older, one a twin. They had grown up in Jacksonville, Illinois. After Betty finished high school, her father, a professor, had gotten a job at Pueblo Junior College in Colorado. The whole family had moved west, including Betty, who enrolled at the college. She explained that she was in Chicago for the summer with her older sister, Shirley, working at Compton Encyclopedia to earn some spending money for school.

As for me, I told her about living in Tehran, about going to the Olympics, about moving to America. In all, we talked for an hour and a half before making the long drive back to the Girls' Club. She was a good listener, easygoing.

When the date was over, I asked Betty if I could call her again, and she agreed.

After all that, we never did go to the dance that Anastasia had cornered me about. It turned out neither one of us was much of a dancer. But it didn't matter; I had bigger plans. I knew after that very first date that Betty was the girl for me. She was everything I'd hoped for: kind, smart, hard-working, honest, pretty, funny, easygoing, uncomplicated, and sassy enough to keep things interesting. She was *stable*. She didn't smoke, didn't drink. So I didn't waste much time; we met in June and were married in August, before Betty was due back at school (she never did go back), and before her parents, Lloyd and Virginia, could do anything about it.

The wedding was small, intimate. We were married on a Wednesday afternoon, on the 19th to be exact, in a Methodist church on Chicago's north side. It reminded me of my church in Iran. I'd always believed in a church wedding; I'd never wanted to stand in front of some random judge to be pronounced man and wife, and Betty, a Unitarian, agreed. I wore my best suit, blue, with a tie, and Betty wore a new blue dress we'd bought at Marshall Field's the week before. She carried a small bouquet of red and white flowers. Our only witnesses were Betty's sister Shirley and her husband, Ken, who was a photographer and took all our pictures.

I hadn't told my brother Sam about the wedding. Sam and his wife, Susie, were forever trying to fix me up, and it drove me nuts. I felt it was none of their business. In fact, nobody in my family knew about the ceremony until after it was over. My mother was disappointed when she found out; she'd always hoped I'd marry a nice Armenian girl. But she got over it. Once she got to know Betty, Mother couldn't help but like her.

After the ceremony, we ate prime rib at the old Ivanhoe restaurant, a few blocks south of Wrigley Field on Clark Street, where we met up with some friends from the Ambassador East. The outside of the Ivanhoe, which opened as a speakeasy during the 1920s but had since evolved into one of the finest restaurants in town, looked like a castle; and the inside was a spectacular dining room. Among the Ivanhoe's more interesting features was a subterranean bar some 300 feet underground. You could see why the whole spread was called "The Seventh Wonder of Chicago" in its day. The Ivanhoe would later become a dinner theatre, then just a theatre, then a liquor store; sadly, it was eventually demolished.

It was a great night. Wonderful. I couldn't have been happier.

When Betty's parents got wind of our wedding, they were a little upset, a bit shocked. They weren't angry, exactly; more like let down. Naturally, they didn't know a thing about me except that I was from Iran, which was a disappointment — especially to Betty's grandfather, who was a proud veteran, and who had wanted Betty to marry a nice American boy. Years later, I discovered that Betty's older sister and husband had called the FBI on me to make sure I was who I said I was, that I hadn't left multiple wives and kids back in the Middle East, that I wasn't a terrorist or something. They were terrified that I'd spirit Betty back to Iran and make her wear a chador — even though Western dress was the fashion of the day under the shah.

Being married to Betty was just as lovely as dating her had been. We made our first home together in a basement apartment, where you could see people's feet as they walked by. Before long, Betty became pregnant with our first child, so we rented a two-bedroom place on Wilson Avenue to accommodate our growing family. As it turned out, though, that apartment had several squatters: cockroaches. I thought I could block all their entrances; for two months I patched the cracks and painted the walls, but still they came. So we moved again, this time to a flat in a Polish neighborhood near Diversey and Crawford; soon thereafter, in September 1960, our daughter Rita was born.

I was thrilled about becoming a father, and I made a point to participate in Rita's day-to-day care — feeding her and changing her diapers. Sure, I was a bit overwhelmed by the added responsibility parenthood entailed, but Rita was so beautiful, such a little miracle, such an easy baby, she made the adjustment a snap.

With my lovely wife and beautiful daughter, my life couldn't have been better. There was just one thing: the weather.

Chicago is known for many things: its fine architecture, its cultural offerings, its shopping. It's a fantastic city, truly, and I had come to love it. But the weather, well, it *sucked*. Swelteringly hot in the summer, unbearably cold in the winter, and not much better in between. For a guy who liked tennis, there weren't many opportunities to play. Tennis was pretty much out of the question from October through April thanks to the cold weather, heavy snow, and blustering winds. I once spent four hours shoveling a public court in the dead of winter just so I could hit a ball around. But I had another reason — a new reason — to leave Chicago: Rita. I'd gotten it in my head that I would teach Rita to play tennis starting at an absurdly young age, and I just didn't think it could be done in the Midwest.

So Betty and I talked it over, and decided to try our luck in Los Angeles. I knew that Southern California was the tennis player's Mecca, that it tended to produce more nationally ranked players than any other region of the country — in part because virtually all the courts in the area, both in the exclusive tennis clubs and in the public parks, were composed of concrete. In those days, private clubs back east maintained grass courts, and public park courts tended to be clay; that meant public park players were at a disadvantage during tournaments because they were unfamiliar with the grass surface. In Los Angeles, however, everyone used the same surface, so no one gained an unfair advantage. The pool of good players was thus effectively doubled, and the likelihood of a public park player acting as a spoiler increased exponentially. A prime example was Pancho Gonzalez, who learned to play on the courts of L.A.'s Exposition Park, and later became one of the greatest players — some would say *the* greatest player — of his era. If I wanted to play tennis, and if I wanted to teach Rita to play, Los Angeles was the place to be.

As it turned out, the Ambassador Hotel chain had a property there, and they were happy to give me a job. So we said goodbye to Sam and Susie and Shirley and Ken, packed up our things, crammed Rita into our four-door, six-cylinder Chevy Impala, navigated to Route 66, and steered west. Back then, I could drive 36 hours straight, no problem, so we made good time — that is, until the engine block busted. After what seemed like an eternity, the car was bandaged up, and we continued on our way.

When we arrived in Los Angeles, things didn't go as I'd hoped. We found a place to live, but it was 60 miles from my job; anything closer was well out of our budget. Yet, our rent nevertheless ran $148 a month, which in those days was a lot; to earn that much, you had to work a week or more. Plus, with all the driving I'd have to do to and from my job, we'd need a new car each year! We made a go of things for a few months, but eventually decided we just couldn't stay.

By then, a friend of mine from Chicago had moved to San Francisco. I rang him up, and he suggested we move north to the Bay area. "Maybe we can find you a job," he said. So Betty (who was then expecting our second child), Rita, and I piled into the car for a second time and steered north on Highway 101. We stayed for two days, approaching every restaurant we could find, but there was nothing available job-wise. And so, demoralized and more than a little weary, we piled into the car yet again and headed back to Chicago. I was bummed out — especially when we arrived and found snow on the ground. On the plus side, I was welcomed back at the Ambassador East with open arms.

After a few months, in the winter of 1962, I had an idea. Phil Boddy, the old maitre d' at the Ambassador East, had signed on as the dining room director at the Tropicana Hotel in Las Vegas. It wasn't Los Angeles, but I knew the weather would be dry and warm, that I'd be able to play tennis 330 days a year if I wanted to.

So one day I called him.

"I can give you a job," he said. "Move here! It's a good place to live."

As soon as he said that, I quit my job at the hotel. As always, Betty was game, so we unloaded everything from the storage room we'd rented upon our return, packed up the car once more, and lumbered off toward Vegas — this time with one additional passenger: our son Phillip, just eight days old.

CHAPTER FIVE

"There are a lot of similarities between poker and tennis.
Both take a lot of patience and discipline. You set up your
opponent and move him around in order to win."
— Jan Fischer, Professional Poker Player

There are few instances when the words "Las Vegas" and "Tehran" can reasonably be spoken in the same breath. Culturally, they are worlds apart — Vegas wears the moniker "Sin City" proudly, while Tehran clings to positively medieval notions of Muslim virtue. Also, Tehran is considerably larger and more populous than Vegas. Topographically, however, Iran is quite similar to Nevada. About half of Iran is covered by desert, wasteland, and barren mountain ranges; ditto Nevada. In Las Vegas, if I squint my eyes and look toward the brown scrubby mountains in the distance (with my back to the Strip, of course), I can almost imagine I'm in Tehran again.

And so, as we tore across the Mojave Desert on the last leg of our journey, I could not help but feel I was finally coming home. Steering my way to the Tropicana, I took in the Strip: the Riviera, the Stardust, the Desert Inn, the Sands, the Flamingo Hotel, the Sahara, the Dunes, the Castaway, the Tally Ho, all set apart like great gapped teeth. The whole street was lit up like an airport runway. I saw no evidence of the wild grasses and plentiful water spied by the traders who first stumbled upon this oasis in the desert and who christened the city Las Vegas, Spanish for "the meadows," in 1829.

And the headliners! Giant marquee letters advertised perform-ances by such luminaries as Dean Martin, Frank Sinatra, Sammy Davis, Jr., Doris Day, Don Rickles, Buddy Hackett, Shecky Greene, Alan King, Louis Prima, and Tony Bennett. (I would, in time, meet just about every headliner who came through town, including the Rat Pack. It just came with the territory when you worked at the casinos.) And of course, there were the shows — *The Lido* at the Stardust, *Minsky's Follies* at the Dunes, *Les Folies Bergère* at the Tropicana.

Las Vegas was no longer the Mormon fort it had been in 1855, when Brigham Young sent 30 missionaries to stake out the valley and to teach the local Paiute Indians how to farm. The Paiutes pre-ferred raiding the fort to farming, prompting the Mormons to rethink their mission; they pulled out in 1857. Likewise, the valley was no longer the farm belt it had become in 1885, after the State Land Act parceled out property at $1.25 per acre. Las Vegas had even outgrown its railroad-town roots, which had sprouted in 1905 when the last piece of track linking Southern California with Salt Lake City was laid. By 1962, Las Vegas housed 22 percent of Nevada's population in a 25-square-mile tract of land, and gaming, which had been legalized by the state in 1931, had become the region's dominant industry.

Finally, I spotted the Tropicana's sign, a 60-foot tulip with flashing pink and aqua neon, and pulled in. Betty stayed in the car with the babies while I ran inside. Immediately, I sensed the allure of the

Tropicana, which had opened in 1957. Unlike other hotels on the Strip, which focused on their casino business, the Tropicana was a hotel *first* and a casino *second* — for example, to ensure that the guests were well cared for, the Tropicana boasted more than one employee per guest — and this distinction showed in its clientele. And unlike most other places in town, the Tropicana was *not* run by the mafia, although it had been tainted by mob connections in earlier days. Former casino manager J.K. Houssels had bought out the original owner, Ben Jaffe, and was known for running a clean operation.

Although the Tropicana placed more emphasis on its being a hotel, that didn't mean the casino was a morgue. In fact, the din of the casino was deafening. As I made my way to the front desk to locate Phil Boddy, I heard yelling and cheering, and the incessant jangling of slots. I'd never been a gambling man, but even my pulse increased from the excitement. (I would, over the next several weeks, piss away the $12,000 I'd brought with us from Chicago on the casino floor; barring the occasional pull of a Megabucks slot machine, I never gambled after that.)

Phil was not there, but he'd left word with his assistant that I could start work the next day. On my first shift, I made $27 in tips — not bad at the time. Before long, I was making $150 a week, which was plenty to cover our expenses. After a few weeks, we moved out of the motel room on Boulder Highway we'd called home and into an apartment on Polaris Drive. It was better than the one I'd grown up in, but not by much; Betty described the windowless flat as "dungeon-like," which was pretty apt.

Called "The Tiffany of the Strip," the Tropicana, a $15-million, 34-acre, 450-room property decorated with a tropical theme, featured an Olympic-size pool in the courtyard surrounded by formal gardens. Overlooking this tropical setting were guest rooms, each with their own private lanais. Across the street was an 18-hole golf course.

There were also two concrete tennis courts — but no pro.

Soon after I started working there, I tracked down the resort's entertainment director, Harvey Dieterich, to ask if I could use the courts to give lessons to hotel guests and to anyone else looking for instruction.

"Do you know how to play?" he asked.

"Yes," I said. "A little."

"I can't give you a salary," he said.

"That's okay," I replied. "I don't want one."

So he agreed. "If you're willing to maintain the courts — keep them clean and whatnot — you can use them."

The first thing I did was hose down and scrub the courts, which Mr. Dieterich liked.

Not long after that, Mr. Dieterich asked me to evaluate a hotel guest's game. The guest was a man named Armando, maybe 40 years old, resplendent in his tennis whites. I'd never seen him before, but as he walked toward me to introduce himself, I could tell by his stride that he was a very good player. He was slightly pigeon-toed, light on his feet, and fast. Twitchy. Andre walks the same way.

"Let's go play some," Armando said to me.

"You are a good player," I said. "I can tell. I'm not going to play a game with you, but I'll hit around. First, though, can I ask you one thing?"

"Sure," he replied.

"What was your best ranking?"

He was stunned. "How did you know?"

"I can tell by your walk," I said. "So tell me. What was your best ranking?"

"I once reached the quarterfinals at Wimbledon," he replied.

Ah, I recognized him now. He was Armando Vieira, the Brazilian tennis star. That made sense. We hit around a while, and of course, his game far surpassed mine. Even so, he spoke well of me to Dieterich.

"He's not a great player," explained Armando, "but he knows *how* to *play*."

I couldn't have said it better myself.

Betty always jokes that our marriage has survived as long as it has — 45 years now — simply because she worked days and I worked nights, and she's probably right. Not long after we arrived in Vegas, Betty found a job working for the State of Nevada as an alien certification specialist — a position she would keep for 28 years before finally retiring in 1992. Basically, her job was to process applications for employers who wished to hire non-citizens, to assess the wage being offered by the employer, and to determine whether any U.S. jobs were at risk as a result of the hire. In any case, she watched Rita and Phillip every night while I worked the dining room at the hotel, and I watched them during the day while she was at the office. We'd see each other for a few minutes each evening and every day at lunch. As for me, I barely slept; I'd get back from the dining room around 3:00 a.m. and sleep until 7:00 a.m. or so before lugging the kids to the courts at the Tropicana.

I'd started giving lessons almost immediately after approaching Mr. Dieterich about using the courts, undercutting the local competition by charging $12 per hour instead of the going rate of $25. Whatever I earned, I put aside.

Early on, I had the brilliant idea to buy a ball machine. I figured I could rent it out to guests so they could practice what they'd learned. Plus, I'd also be able to use it when I taught, which meant I wouldn't have to run around so much. Problem was, at the time, I didn't have enough money to buy one. I called a manufacturer rep and asked if I could buy a machine on credit. His answer: No way. I didn't give up, though. I convinced the guy to check out my operation at the Tropicana. Finally, he agreed. After he saw that I was serious, he arranged to sell me a machine on credit — $150 down, and three more payments of $150 each to follow.

The machine was great, but I noticed that it could use some improvements. I'd always been pretty mechanically inclined, so I tinkered with it a little so it would spit out more balls per session, more quickly, and with a bit of topspin. Pretty soon, I had earned enough money to pay off the manufacturer *and* buy more machines. I tinkered with those machines, too, modifying them to throw different shots — outside-in shots, inside-out shots, slices, lobs, and so on — all at different frequencies. I even modified a ball machine to serve; it was seven feet tall, and shot the balls out at a speed of 98 miles per hour. (As an aside, after word of my innovations spread, I eventually consulted with various ball-machine companies, including Matchmate and Playmate, to show them how to add functionality to their machines the way I had.)

I was able to rent out each machine for $12 an hour. As a result, on top of what I made working the dining room, I was pulling in about $50 a day on the courts. It wasn't millions, but it was enough to buy a better life for me and my family. In 1966, we bought our first home, a three-bedroom tract house on El Segundo in a family neighborhood, just down the street from former heavyweight champ Sonny Liston. His family was the only black family in the neighborhood, and because I suspected our neighbors weren't thrilled about their arrival, I made a point to walk over and introduce myself. I knew what it felt like to be an outsider. He was nice, but he kept to himself.

Anytime I had a break in my lessons, I taught Rita, who was two when we arrived in Vegas, to play. I figured, I have a daughter, I have a son; they could be world champion singles, world champion mixed doubles. That was what I was shooting for.

Of course, in those days, it was unheard of to teach a toddler to play tennis — a girl, no less. The prevailing wisdom was to wait until kids were bigger, stronger, before introducing them to the game. Billie Jean King didn't start until she was 11; Bobby Riggs started at 12. But I thought, the earlier you start, the better. Tennis becomes part of the kids' lives. Their walk becomes a tennis walk. Their thinking becomes tennis thinking. You start them early, they become great. They might not become No. 1 in the world, but they'll become the best player they can be. So as soon as Rita could wrap her tiny hands around a racket, we went to work.

Why? Good question. Partly because becoming world champion was a goal I'd never reached. In boxing, I'd had the ability, the gift, but for various reasons — birthplace, financial situation — I didn't make it. The same is true with tennis. For me, the next best thing was seeing my kids achieve that dream.

But there was something else. You see, I had a vision. Not a

"Joan of Arc" vision or a "Moses and the burning bush" vision. Rather, mine was about tennis. The way I saw it, tennis could be *big*. It could fill stadiums from Dubai to Duluth. It could transcend social strata, could attract players and fans from every nation on Earth. And as tennis grew, so, too, would the amount of money a top player could net — I guessed in the millions.

Sounds crazy, right? After all, in the early 1960s, there was no ATP or WTA circuit like we have today. Instead, pros signed with promoters, who paid them a pittance to travel the globe, playing match after match — often more than 100 in all — against the same opponent, after which the world champion would be crowned. Grand Slam events were held each year at the Australian, French, Wimbledon, and U.S. Championships, but at that time were open only to amateurs.

And as for that increase in popularity among tennis watchers? Lunacy. In the 1960s, tennis was hardly a game for the masses. It was played and followed primarily by the wealthy, by country-clubbers who wore white V-neck cable-knit sweaters and used too much hair pomade. Sure, the occasional rebel pro came along and stirred things up — Pancho Gonzalez comes to mind — but overall, tennis just didn't offer much for the average Joe.

The main problem with tennis was that it was, well, a bit boring. It was slow. Each player stood sideways at the baseline and waited for the ball to bounce and crest before swatting at it from underneath with a locked wrist, a straight arm, and a long follow-through. It took so long, you practically had time to catch a movie between shots. At the very least, players had plenty of time to think, to strategize, to plan their next move.

But I had a theory: I figured if you could speed up that return

— by hitting the ball sooner, by hitting it harder, or both — you could make it much more difficult for your opponent to retrieve it. The game would become faster, more exciting, and by extension, more popular and more lucrative.

So my goal wasn't to teach Rita, to teach all my kids, the fundamentals of the game as it stood in the 1960s and 1970s. Rather, I meant to teach my kids the game of the future.

Moreover, I intended to *shape* that future.

If speed and power were key, and I was certain they were, the question was, how does one learn to play with speed and power, yet maintain some level of accuracy? In those days, the party line was to teach kids to hit accurately first, and *then* to teach them to increase their power. I took the opposite approach. My answer was to teach the kids to hit the ball early and hard — as hard as their little bodies allowed — precision be damned. Once they had that down, they honed their accuracy through practice. And by practice, I mean hitting *thousands* of balls a week. I figured you had to do it every day, and each day better than the one before; otherwise, you were wasting your time. My first three kids hit somewhere between 7,000 and 8,000 balls a week; Andre hit almost twice that number. Once, I sat down and did the math: That's nearly a million balls a year. Thank God I'd bought those ball machines.

The kids would hit the same shot over and over, sometimes for days on end or even over a period of years, until it became instinct. Then they'd vary the shot, hitting it a shorter distance, a deeper distance, from the middle of the court, from behind the baseline. And because a player is only as strong as his weakest shot, I made sure the kids practiced this way for every type of stroke — forehand, backhand, volley, overhead, you name it. That way, anytime they were dealt a particular shot in a match, wherever they were on the court, they knew in their very bones how to return it with pace and accuracy.

That instinct, I believed, would become critical if my predictions about the game were accurate — that is, if tennis evolved from a chess-like game in which players had time to think, strategize, and plan their shots, into a game in which players hit the ball early, on the rise, and with tremendous power. If the game sped up like I thought it would, players simply wouldn't have time to weigh their decisions on the court. Their bodies would need to respond mechanically, without the intervention of thought.

I, however, was *always* thinking. I studied other sports to see what I could apply to my kids' games. For example, I knew from my own experience as a boxer that in order to pepper a punch, you must snap your wrist. I suspected the same technique could be applied to a tennis racket to increase pace and power, and I was right.

I watched football, and noticed the way a quarterback packs more power into a throw by hurling the ball slightly side-armed. Because the throwing motion is not terribly unlike the service motion in tennis, I wondered if moving the serve stroke slightly to the side would improve the serve's speed and power. It did.

I noticed that during their swing, baseball players, in addition to putting their whole bodies into the motion, snap both their wrist and their hip to generate torque, and I found that the motion transferred well to a forehand stroke — even the way they sometimes end up with their weight on their back foot. It ended up helping my kids power their strokes.

Even bowling was instructive, the way a simple flick of the bowler's wrist could spin a ball to within millimeters of the gutter and then reel it back to the center pin.

And of course, I studied tennis. I'd watch the ball's speed, its spin, and try to determine just what a player did to make it so. Every so often, a player would tweak his shot, sometimes unintentionally, and I'd note the results. Take Ivan Lendl. Once I saw him hit the ball on the rise — *once*. It was probably the only time in his life that he did it. Same with Bjorn Borg. A few times, in a match, Borg hit the ball earlier than normal. But I saw it, I saw how it mixed things up for their opponents, and I put that into my children's games. It was almost Darwinian, the way I analyzed the game; a minor deviation in one player's technique could yield an entirely new sub-species of shot, even a new type of tennis entirely. I also analyzed what made other players great, and tried to assemble a sort of montage of skills in my own kids. I thought I could take a little of Lendl, some Borg, and a dash of McEnroe to create an unbeatable Frankenplayer.

Rita calls herself the guinea pig in my grand tennis experiment, and she's right — especially when you consider that as subjects of experimentation, guinea pigs are often destroyed. It sounds melodramatic, I know, but there are times I wish I'd never put a racket in her hand. I paid such a price; we all did.

The fact is, I ruined tennis for Rita — ruined her life, really — by pushing her too hard. I made sure it was tennis all the time. When Rita's friends were at the movies, out having a good time, Rita was on the tennis court — always.

Rita *hated* it. She wanted to enjoy tennis, she liked to play, but she hated being pushed, and she hated me for doing it. Eventually, she had enough; any time I pushed her, she pushed right back, even throwing games and sometimes entire matches to make her point. I believe to this day that she could have been better than Martina Navratilova, who was four years older, better than Billie Jean King, better than *anyone*, but she never wanted it — probably because I did. She was determined to live her own life, not the one I'd designed for her.

Slow learner that I am, I made the same mistake with my second child, Phillip. Unlike Rita, Phillip wasn't particularly competitive by nature and, I suspect, wasn't terribly interested in the game. He would get rattled, especially in high-pressure matches. The way I saw it, if you're love-40 behind, come out swinging with four winners! That's what Andre does. When he's losing, he goes for broke, and usually it works. But Phillip just wasn't that way. He didn't have that killer instinct. He's simply a nice guy, you know? And I imagine my constant haranguing didn't do much for his confidence. Nevertheless, he developed a fine game, with a serve that was even bigger than Andre's ended up being.

When my third child, Tami, arrived on the scene in 1969, I followed a slightly different approach. As unhappy as Rita had become by then, as angry as she was at me, I knew I'd already lost one daughter, and I didn't want to lose another. So I didn't push Tami the way I did Rita and Phillip. I taught her to play, of course, but I didn't demand that she do it to the exclusion of all other things. If she wanted to play, fine. If not, that was fine too. As it turned out, Tami enjoyed the game, although she wasn't terribly competitive by nature.

By the time Andre was born on April 29, 1970, I was ready. I vowed that I wouldn't push him the way I had Rita and Phillip. I would, however, begin teaching him about tennis before he could walk, before he could talk, before he could even *sit*. I figured if he took to the game, then we would work from there; if not, so be it.

I had read somewhere that the first muscle a baby develops is the one that allows him to focus his eyes. And so, even before my new baby boy was released from Sunrise Hospital in Las Vegas, I designed a special mobile for his crib that consisted of a tennis ball dangling from a wooden Garcia tennis racket. After we brought Andre home, each time any of us passed by his crib, we tapped the racket to make the ball swing back and forth; and each time we did, Andre's eyes — those *huge* eyes — would follow that ball. My theory was that as Andre grew older, the sight of a tennis ball coming his way would be familiar.

I also believed I could hardwire Andre's body to swing a racket, to make contact with a secondary object, and in doing so, boost his hand-eye coordination. Therefore, when Andre was six or seven months old, I developed a special game in which I put him in his high chair, dangled a balloon over him, and let him whack at it with a ping-pong paddle.

Later, when he started using a walker, I gave him the same Garcia racket that had once hung over his crib; with great accuracy and pace, he used it to line-drive a salt shaker through a glass door. When Andre began walking on his own, I took him outside and tossed tennis balls at him. Racket in hand, he'd chase them down and swing away; soon, he began playing on his own against the playroom wall. When he got tired, he'd put the ball under his racket and use it as a pillow and take a nap. Then he'd wake up and start to hit again.

By the time Andre turned three, I had taught him the basic strokes: a two-handed backhand, a one-handed forehand. At four, Andre had a complete game. He could serve, he could volley. He could do it all. And at six, the kid could return anything you threw at him.

You can buy the most expensive cars, you can buy a mansion, you can buy a tennis court, you can buy the best equipment, but you cannot buy talent, you cannot buy desire. With Andre, that was never a concern. He wasn't just the most talented of my four kids, he was the most willing. I'd go so far as to say that by a certain age, *he* drove *me*. Bottom line: Andre was easier to coach than my other kids had been. He had the desire. I don't know if it was the desire to play tennis, or if it was simply the desire to please me, but he had it.

Andre quickly became somewhat of a local phenomenon. Because of my contacts in the casinos, I was able to convince the organizers of the yearly Alan King tennis tournament at Caesar's Palace to include Andre in a few exhibition matches. Once, he hit around with Bobby Riggs in front of 50 or so slack-jawed spectators. Despite his defeat at the hands of Billie Jean King in the Battle of the Sexes a few years earlier, Bobby was a great sport with Andre, and the two put on quite a show. Andre, who was in diapers at the time, would come to the net and lob over Bobby's head, Bobby would run back to return it, and Andre would nail him with a perfect drop shot. Playing with Riggs is one of Andre's earliest memories.

I introduced Andre to many of the tournament players, and persuaded Jimmy Connors to hit around with my son on Andre's fourth birthday. After a session with Ilie Nastase, Andre signed his first autograph. He was six years old. At eight, Andre rallied with Bjorn Borg. Once, tournament organizers gathered a half-dozen pros to play for charity; benefactors could pay money in order to play a set with a pro. After paying $100, one guy got Andre to play in his place. Andre played Harold Solomon, who, during the course of his pro career, claimed 22 singles titles; when they were finished, the crowd cheered so loudly that Solomon offered to play one more set with Andre. "He has a better backhand than *I* do!" Solomon exclaimed. Andre was nine at the time.

Andre became so big, so known, that the minute the pros arrived at Caesar's, the first thing out of their mouths was "Where's Andre?"

Where was Andre? He was practicing. Always.

CHAPTER SIX

"That'll wake up the country club."

— Andre Agassi

The overzealous tennis parent: It's a cliché, really. Practically every player on the tour — man and woman — has at least one parent who is or acts like a certifiable lunatic. Take Jim Pierce, father of former WTA standout Mary Pierce. After punching two fans at the 1992 French Open, he was banned from all tour matches. His behavior even prompted the WTA to institute a new rule, the "Jim Pierce" rule, which prohibits players, coaches, and relatives from acting in an abusive manner. Damir Dokic, Jelena Dokic's father, is another, having been banned from attending tournaments after several run-ins with tournament officials and police. At one Wimbledon tune-up in 1999, he was ejected from the stands for drunk and disorderly conduct; later that day, he was arrested for lying down in the middle of a roadway. In 2000, he smashed a journalist's mobile phone at Wimbledon and was forcibly removed from the grounds of Flushing Meadows after becoming enraged over the price of his meal. (Then again, those concessions people do rob you blind sometimes.)

It's no different at the junior level. Take the baffling case of Frenchman Christophe Fauviau, who was recently accused of using antidepressants to spike the drinks of his 16-year-old son's opponents, including Alexandre Lagardere, who died after falling asleep behind the wheel while driving home from his match.

I'd like to state for the record that I was never *that* bad.

I admit I developed a bit of a reputation as a tyrant during the years my children were playing in the juniors. I'm not saying I didn't deserve it; I suspect I did. But I had dreams for my kids, and I was determined to do everything I could to see them come true. I knew education was important, so I forced my kids to go to school; likewise, tennis was important, so I forced them to play. Sometimes they wanted to, sometimes they didn't, but always they played. After each match, I'd corner them to discuss how things went; I could remember every point. They didn't like that. Rita once said, "I won! Leave me alone!" But I wanted to analyze each point to help them improve.

The way I see it, a kid's success, more often than not, depends on his parents. It's because of his parents that a child becomes successful in sports, successful in life. Parents (and other relatives) are the greatest teachers in the world. Take Jimmy Connors. He learned the game from his mother and his grandmother. They taught him to be great. The Williams sisters learned the game from their father, Richard Williams. Steffi Graf's father quit his job as a used-car salesman to nurture his daughter's talent. Monica Seles's dad, who was a cartoonist, used to motivate her to play by drawing funny pictures on the balls. Ivan Lendl learned from his father and his mother, both nationally ranked Czech players. Pierce, Dokic; they might have gone off the deep end, but you can bet their daughters would have never cracked the top ten if they hadn't dedicated every ounce of their being to coaching.

As for me, it seemed like my efforts with my own kids were continuously thwarted by the USTA, by the tournament directors, by the other parents. For starters, our region included Nevada, Utah, Wyoming, Colorado, and Montana, but not California. I ceaselessly nagged the USTA to fold Nevada into California's region — one, it was closer, and two, it tended to offer better competition — but they refused. So week after week, I'd get off from work on Friday, load the kids in the car, and drive all the way to Salt Lake City — 500 miles in all — where most of their tournaments were held. We'd get there at 11:00 p.m., fall into bed, and wake back up in time to get everybody to their events — which, you could be sure, were never at the same club. Rita's would be at one club, and Phillip's would be at another, and Andre's would be across town. They'd be exhausted before they even stepped on the court. But those kids from Salt Lake, they could just roll out of bed and mosey on over, fresh, rested, and ready to go.

But okay. That's the way it goes. I could live with that. What really got to me was when my kids started becoming victims of sabotage. It was like there was a tennis Mafia or something. When Rita was 16, I bought her a 1977 Chrysler Cordova and gave her a credit card so she and Phillip could travel on their own. One weekend, they drove to Salt Lake City and were staying at some housing provided by tournament officials, Rita at one site and Phillip at another. While they were there, her tires were slashed! If that weren't enough, someone had broken into the car and stolen all her rackets and her money. She was so dominant in the region, I guess the other kids — or their parents — got desperate. She called home in tears, so I took off from my job, sped to the house, strung two rackets, and drove like an Andretti — 100, 110 miles per hour — to Salt Lake City. I got there at nine in the morning, but couldn't find Rita; meanwhile, the tournament officials were telling me they were going to disqualify her.

"What do you mean disqualify her?" I asked, incredulous.

"She's not here at the assigned time, so we'll have to disqualify her," they said.

"But you're the ones who provided housing for her. Where is she?"

"We don't know," they shrugged. "We're not responsible for her transportation."

As we were talking, a 320-pound truck driver walked in with Rita by his side. She'd had to hitchhike. I handed Rita one of the rackets I'd strung and escorted her to the court. The officials wouldn't let her warm up, and granted Rita's opponent four games because Rita was late. Rita lost the first set 7–5, but claimed the second and third sets to win the match. The next day, both Rita and Phillip won the final, but neither accepted their trophies. They walked off and we came home.

Even when my kids weren't sabotaged directly, I just couldn't shake the feeling that the tournament officials conspired to prevent us from winning. One time, Phillip was playing a semifinal match. At 5–3, Phillip nailed a match point, strode to the net, and shook hands with his opponent, only to have the ball called out by an official who was 80 feet away. None of the other officials, ones who had actually been nearby when the shot occurred, spoke up in our defense. Poor Phillip stalked back to the baseline, but was so angry, so flummoxed, he couldn't hit the broad side of a barn with the ball. His opponent took the game, and the next, and the next, and the *next* to win the match.

That kind of stuff got me hot under the collar.

The thing was, I felt like the USTA and the tournament officials should have been interested in finding the absolute best kids, in fostering their talent, in helping them rise to the top internationally if that's what the child wanted. I mean, as I understood it, that was the whole point of the USTA's existence. But that's not what the USTA did. It always felt like everything was terribly political with them. Nobody cared who was "best"; they had their favorites, and they bent over backwards to make sure those people were the ones who were rewarded.

Once, I took Andre to Houston for a tournament. He wasn't entered, but I knew he was good enough to play, so I figured I'd try to get him in as a wildcard. I found the man in charge and persuaded him to watch Andre play, to let him in the bracket. Before I knew it, other parents started calling the guy and telling him that if he put Andre in the tournament, they would sue. Andre, who should have qualified, probably would have won.

During those years, we spent a *lot* of money on attorneys, fighting off attacks like that one.

The NCAA (National Collegiate Athletic Association) was no better. When Phillip played as the top seed for the University of Nevada, Las Vegas (UNLV), he garnered a 40–3 record. Yet, when it came time to decide who should play in the NCAA tourney, the coaches in Phillip's region voted against him 3–2. Instead, they sent three players who had lost about a dozen matches each, two of whom had lost to Phillip. I felt bad for my son, so I took our grievance to the NCAA and the USTA, with no results. The whole thing reminded me of how the Iranian Olympic Committee tried to un-invite me from the 1948 Olympics, even though I had clearly qualified, but this time there was no shah to make things right.

So yes, I was angry a lot of the time. My priority was looking out for my kids, making sure they didn't get screwed by the system, and I suspect that seemed pretty rude to many of the other parents — even though they were doing the same thing for their own children. For example, like many parents, I coached my kids from the stands. We'd worked out some hand signals, and I spent half their matches twitching like a third-base coach. Because of me, though, coaching during matches became illegal. Why? Our kids were beating everyone. It wasn't because of my coaching; they'd have won either way. But the tournament officials certainly didn't want to give us any advantage. After that, anyplace I went, there'd be three other parents around me to make sure I didn't break the rule. I could have farted, and they'd have accused me of coaching.

Perhaps it was just a cultural difference. Not to generalize, but Middle Easterners, including yours truly, do tend to be pretty aggressive, which just isn't *done* at country clubs. The whole thing reminds me of that bus ride I took on my first visit to London, the one where the interpreter told us how to behave, not to spit or litter on the street. Maybe if I'd had a guide when my kids first started playing, I'd have done a little better. You know, "Smile nicely when you stab people in the back" or "Shake hands with the other parents after a match in the spirit of fair play, even if fair play has not occurred" — that kind of thing. But that wasn't my way of doing things. When I saw something was wrong, I spoke up! I ranted. I accosted officials when I felt they'd cheated my kids. I pissed off the other parents by being loud, but worse, for daring to question their authority, and to confront them when I felt we'd been wronged. Once, after Andre had been cheated out of a match by some atrocious line calls, I told the person running the tournament that one day, he would beg me to let my son play Davis Cup for them. He laughed at me. They all did. But years later, when I was watching Andre play a Davis Cup match in Germany, that same guy came up to me, smiled, and said, "Remember what you told me?"

Yeah, I remembered. I *never* forgot.

As bad as all that political crap is at the junior level, it's worse the higher up the ladder you go. Even the Grand Slams play unfairly when it comes to matters like distributing wildcard berths. At the French Open, for example, the wildcards tend to go to French players. Either that or negotiations will ensue, as in "We'll let in two Aussies at Roland Garros if you'll let in two of our guys at the next Australian Open." That works great for Australia and France, but what about everybody else? I think that those berths should be distributed based on ability. I mean, the whole point of a Grand Slam is to showcase the best players in the world, and if you don't let people in who have earned the right to be there, then why bother? Even better, nix the wildcard altogether. Just make certain that previous Grand Slam winners are eligible, slot in the top 16, and make everybody else play a qualifying round. That way, there are no hard feelings. Really, the best way to solve the problem is to create one federation for the game, the way FIFA runs soccer and FIS handles skiing; you at least increase the odds that tournaments get run fairly and that they get promoted the way they should. I doubt, though, that any of these types of changes will be instigated. Tennis will just go on the way it has been — steadily losing viewers and sponsors to games like golf.

At the junior level, part of the problem was that the tournaments were run primarily by a clique of parents — and if you weren't in the clique, you could bet that your kid would be screwed. Needless to say, the Agassis were not in the clique. Maybe it was just because my kids were so much better than everyone else's, or maybe it was a caste thing. Most of these parents were doctors or lawyers or college professors or CEOs, and here I was, this upstart casino worker. And of course, I was from Iran, which, especially during the 1979 hostage crisis, didn't exactly win me any friends.

Iran had suffered a terrible decline in the years since I'd left. After leaving the country in the early 1950s, the shah garnered support from Great Britain, the United States, France, and the Netherlands in order to stage his return. In exchange, the shah permitted an international consortium of companies to manage Iran's oil industry for the next 25 years — with all profits going to the consortium and none to Iran. Not surprisingly, this arrangement was not to the liking of many of the shah's subjects.

Then, in the early 1960s, the shah initiated yet more liberal economic, social, and administrative reforms — reforms that alienated the more conservative religious and political groups. Riots in 1963 and the assassination of Premier Hassan Ali Mansur in 1965 prompted a crackdown by the shah's dreaded secret police, the SAVAK. By the early 1970s, the shah suffered from widespread religious and political opposition, which only continued to grow. In early 1979, the shah saw the writing on the wall and "took a vacation" (that is, fled for his life). In his absence, the Ayatollah Khomeini launched the

Islamic Revolution, which ended with the creation of a theocratic republic guided by Islamic principles. It goes without saying that the new government was extremely conservative and fervently anti-Western. Those who favored the shah learned to lie low or perish.

In 1979, militant Iranian students, furious that the shah had been permitted to receive medical treatment in America (they demanded that he be returned to face trial) and generally peeved over the United States' support of the shah's regime, raided the U.S. Embassy in Tehran and took 66 hostages. After months of fruitless efforts to free the hostages, President Jimmy Carter severed diplomatic ties and imposed a complete economic embargo on Iran.

I can't say that I blamed him, but this was bad news for my family members who still lived there. Things only got worse for them when neighboring nation Iraq started lobbing missiles over the border, marking the commencement of a war that would endure for eight years.

Fortunately, though, by 1979, most of us surviving Agassis had left Iran for good, forging our destinies in America. My sister, Helen, had the good fortune to marry an American Lutheran minister who had served as a missionary in Tehran. They settled in Belvedere, Illinois, in 1959. As for my mother, she got her hands on a visitor's visa in 1969 after my father died, and spent the next 11 years alternating between living with Betty, me, and the kids in Las Vegas and with Helen in Illinois. (Mom passed away in 1980.) My brothers Issar and Helmut, however, weren't so lucky.

Issar had become very wealthy in Iran over the years during the shah's reign, ultimately becoming the head of an oil refinery. But when the Revolution arrived and the refinery was taken over by the new government, he knew he had to flee — just like my father had done after the White Army fell to the Bolsheviks all those years before. After paying off the appropriate corrupt government officials, Issar, with his wife and daughter in tow, left in the night, bound for Pakistan en route to America. I was thrilled to see him — I'd always adored Issar — but he couldn't find decent work. Nobody seemed interested in hiring an Iranian to do the type of work for which he was qualified. He died from the stress a few years later.

Sadly, Issar wasn't the first of my siblings to die. Some years earlier, in 1972, my brother Sam was killed when the canoe he was paddling rushed over a dam. I'd been close to Sam, and his death was horrible for us all. It was hard to believe the proud young man who'd picked me up at the train station when I arrived in Chicago was gone.

As for Helmut, he was stuck. He'd actually moved to America in 1962, but, seduced by Issar's success in Iran, had returned to Tehran in 1970. Helmut is about the only guy I know who left America for Iran, but there you have it. He made a go of things for a while, marrying and starting a family, but the Islamic Revolution dashed any hopes he had for prosperity.

By the time she was 13, Rita was hurtling toward tennis burnout. The exacting — some would say tortuous — training regimen I'd developed for her was taking its toll on her *and* on me. She wouldn't listen. She didn't care. To make me unhappy, she'd lose matches on purpose. If I was watching, she'd launch her returns over the fence. As long as I wasn't there, she'd play her game, and she'd usually win. But as soon as I showed up courtside, she'd start tanking. If I wanted to see her match, I had to climb a nearby tree and perch on a sturdy limb, hidden from Rita's view by the foliage. Despite her feelings about the game, when a friend invited her to participate in a clinic at Caesar's Palace given by tennis legend Pancho Gonzalez, Rita figured, why not?

Pancho, who was the new director of tennis at Caesar's, saw Rita's talent immediately.

Even at 13, Rita was amazing. I'd started her on the game as a toddler, much younger than any other girls around, and it paid off. As far as I'm concerned, she was the first woman ever to hit the ball as hard as Venus and Serena Williams do today. She could hit almost as hard as Andre does — which, in 1973, was pretty unusual. She wasn't the quickest girl on the court, but it didn't matter; nobody could rally with her because they couldn't return her shots. She had an unbelievable two-handed weapon on both sides, not unlike the strokes that Monica Seles used so effectively years later.

When I arrived to pick Rita up, Pancho approached me. "How did you teach this girl how to hit?" he asked.

"I used ball machines," I answered. "She practices for hours every day."

He shook his head and whistled. "She's unbelievable," he said.

Against my better judgment, I enlisted Pancho's help with Rita. I say "against my better judgment" because I knew firsthand just what kind of man Pancho was. Back in Chicago, I once served as a line judge during one of his matches. Gonzalez disagreed with a few of my calls and heckled me so spitefully I stalked off the court mid-match. That incident was only one of many for Pancho; as famous as he was for his game, he was perhaps even more famous for his terrible on-court behavior. Once, when a chair umpire refused to overrule an objectionable call, Pancho smashed the man's microphone. Another time, he threw a chair at a referee. If you ask the casual observer to name the most abusive tennis champion in the history of the game, most people would say John McEnroe or Jimmy Connors. No doubt about it, both were famous for their explosive tempers, their abusive tirades. But McEnroe and Connors were bad behavior *lite*. They had *nothing* on Pancho Gonzalez.

Not surprisingly, I wasn't terribly comfortable placing my daughter under the tutelage of such a person, but my back was against the wall. Rita had long since stopped listening to me; if she was to become the tennis champion I knew she could be, she needed outside help. Pancho was my only hope.

It's odd, when you think about it, how many things I had in common with Pancho Gonzalez, especially when you consider how very much I despised him at one time. Like my father, who had endured terrible hardship to escape Russia — traveling by bicycle, mule, and foot to cross into Iran — Pancho's father, Manuel, had walked from Chihuahua, Mexico to Arizona — a distance of some 900 miles — eventually settling in South Central Los Angeles and working as a housepainter. Pancho described his father as a quiet-mannered man who seldom raised his voice, a description that could easily have been applied to my own father.

Both Pancho and I came from large families; he had six brothers and sisters, while I had four. Like us, the Gonzalez clan lived simply. As Pancho wrote in his 1959 autobiography, *Man with a Racket*, "We had few luxuries at our house. Food wasn't abundant, but it was simple and filling, and we never went hungry.

Our clothes were just clothes — inexpensive but clean."

Sound familiar?

The similarities don't stop there. He also chose a name that suited him, opting for "Pancho" over the "Richard" that appeared on his birth certificate. And Pancho had taught himself the fundamentals of tennis — in his case, using a 51-cent racket that his mother had bought him in lieu of the bicycle he'd requested. Similarly, he was the ultimate tennis outsider. He'd honed his game on the eight hard-surfaced public courts of L.A.'s Exposition Park, far from the Los Angeles Tennis Club, the WASP enclave that had spawned most of the better players in the region. Allison Danzig, the famous sportswriter for *The New York Times*, once called Pancho "the rankest outsider of modern times," and he's not far off.

Interestingly enough, Pancho's playing style wasn't unlike Andre's. Both were noted for their quick reflexes, for their street-fighting approach to the game. Pancho, like Andre, hit the crap out of the ball every time it came his way. Likewise, the arc of Pancho's professional tennis career was similar to Andre's. Both showed tremendous promise early in their careers — Pancho prevailing at Forest Hills in 1948 as a 20-year-old to claim the title of United States Singles Champion, Andre making a colossal impression on the pro circuit while still a teenager. And as with Andre, who received tremendous criticism as a young player for his inconsistent style (often due to his laziness and lack of commitment), tennis fans believed Pancho would flame out early — returning, tail between his legs, to the barrio. Indeed, after his tremendous win at Forest Hills, Pancho did get lazy, did rest on his laurels, and proceeded to lose just about every remaining match in 1948 (though he did charge back to reclaim his title at Forest Hills in

1949). In his autobiography, he wrote: "Now the tongues really began to wag. Some began to chant that my title win was a fluke."

When Pancho turned pro in 1949, after enjoying international acclaim as a member of the U.S. Davis Cup team that beat Australia to win the Cup, he was pulverized nightly by his opponent, Jack Kramer. (In those days, pro players didn't have a circuit like they do today; rather, promoters like Bobby Riggs organized tours in which the same two players battled night after night.) Humiliated, Pancho entered semi-retirement — for a time, at least.

Of course, both Pancho and Andre proved the naysayers wrong, each enjoying a long career. At 33, Andre was one of the oldest men in the history of the tour to achieve the ranking of No. 1 in the world in 2003; likewise, Pancho stormed back in 1954, at the age of 26, and staked his claim as the professional champion nine times in a span of 10 years. After another brief retirement in 1963, Gonzalez returned to the court, where he continued winning matches into his 40s — including an unbelievable two-day first-round battle against his protegé Charlie Pasarell at Wimbledon in 1969, which Pancho finally won 22–24, 1–6, 16–14, 6–3, 11–9. The 112-game match, which lasted five hours and 12 minutes, was one major impetus for the institution of the tiebreaker in tennis. In 1971, at the age of 43, Gonzalez would defeat 19-year-old up-and-comer Jimmy Connors at the Pacific Southwest Open.

As impressed as Pancho was with Rita, young Rita was doubly so with Pancho. Whoever invented the phrase "tall, dark, and handsome" almost certainly had Gonzalez in mind. As Vincent Flaherty of the *Los Angeles Examiner* once wrote of Pancho, "The movies haven't a more virile specimen of masculinity. He causes the feminine heartstrings to make like soft chimes."

Well, whatever.

I suspect that Rita was smitten from the moment she met Pancho, who was 32 years her senior. He was born two years before I was! But you see, Pancho, in addition to being a fine physical specimen, had found his way into Rita's heart through the simple act of complimenting her — something I rarely did.

By the time she was 15, I began to suspect that Rita harbored for Pancho something a bit more serious than a crush. I remembered a story from my Chicago days about a school teacher seducing a 15-year-old girl; given what I knew of Pancho's history with women — he was, at that time, on marriage number five, and had fathered seven children — I was worried that Rita would meet the same fate. I demanded that she stop training with Pancho, but she refused. By then, there wasn't much I could do to enforce my rule; he'd given her a job at the pro shop on site at Caesar's that paid $30 a day. Later, he hired her to teach. She became pretty independent. As soon as she turned 18, she moved out. She traveled the satellite circuit for a time with Pancho as her coach, and even cracked the top 100, but eventually retired and went back to teaching.

In 1984, Pancho and Rita married. Rita was 24, Pancho 56.

It goes without saying that I did not attend the ceremony. Betty went, but I stayed away.

After that, Rita was dead to me. I did not speak to her for years. I'd see her at tennis events, but we'd pass without a word. There was a lot of tension, a lot of trouble — for all of us. Nonetheless, Betty never gave up on her. She and Rita still talked, and I was glad about that, relieved that someone in the family was keeping tabs on Rita. But for me, it was over.

Look, the kid was of legal age. It's not like she didn't have the right to do what she wanted. After all, Betty and I had gotten married without our parents' blessings. But I knew — I *knew* — she'd married Pancho just to spite me. She knew how I felt about him. He was a horrible choice for her, far too old and with a terrible track record to boot. But for Rita, marrying Pancho was the ultimate rebellion, the best way she knew to declare her independence from me and to send me a big F.U. along the way. Maybe she loved him too, I don't know. She says she did. But if she did, I think it was that delusional love of youth, the kind you only feel when your hormones are tumbling like clothes in a dryer.

I missed her, of course. She was loud and fiery and a pain in the ass, but she was *my* pain in the ass. But I tried to focus on the positive things in my life — on Andre's success on the junior circuit, and on making sure he realized my dream even if Rita didn't.

CHAPTER SEVEN

"Parents have to stay parents. It never works with a coach who's a mother or father. It's not good for the relationship. There comes a moment when you simply start sending them to hell in your mind."
— Marat Safin, 2000 U.S. Open Champion

Just as Rita had damned me in her teens, so too did Andre. By the time he was 13, he'd stopped listening to me. It didn't take me long to realize that if Andre was going to make it to the ATP tour, he'd need more than I could give him. And so, just as I'd placed Rita under the tutelage of Pancho Gonzalez, unfortunate outcome aside, it was time for me to find a coach for Andre. The problem was there was no one in Vegas to fill the job. Pancho was out for obvious reasons. Besides, Gonzalez didn't think Andre had the goods. "He's a shorty," Pancho jeered. He figured Rita had been my best hope, and by then, she'd already retired.

With regard to his views on Andre, however, Gonzalez was in the minority. A few years earlier, when Andre was 11 or so, we'd taken him to a tournament in San Diego. Tennis legend Pancho Segura happened to catch one of Andre's matches and invited us to his place afterward — along with another man we called Tutti

Frutti because he sold juice all over Southern California. When we arrived, Segura and Tutti Frutti started placing calls all over the greater San Diego area to try to get a game for Andre in the hopes of placing a few bets. I knew where they were coming from; in Segura's pro days, betting sets was how they supplemented their meager tour earnings, but it turned me right off. "My son is not a hustler," I said. Undeterred, Segura offered to play a set against Andre himself — for a friendly wager, of course.

I was curious to see how Andre would fare against Segura. Segura might have entered his twilight years — by then, he was in his 60s — but he was still fit and agile and a master tactician. Nonetheless, I wasn't keen on using Andre like some sort of poker chip, and I didn't have enough money on me anyway — Segura had suggested a wager of $100 to make things more interesting — so I declined. No matter; Tutti Frutti whipped out his overstuffed wallet and plucked out a one-hundred-dollar bill, and the set was on.

There they were, my 11-year-old son on one side of the net, and the 60-something-year-old Pancho Segura on the other. It was one hell of a battle. Andre finally broke Pancho late in the set, but when he served for the win, one of the witnesses called his ball out. It wasn't out, I saw it with my own eyes, but there you have it. Segura went on to win the set 7–5.

Afterward, Segura made us an offer: He'd coach Andre six days a month in exchange for complete control over Andre's development and 12 percent of Andre's future earnings. All we had to do was put Andre on a plane to San Diego 12 times a year, and we had a deal.

As we sat there, I thought it over.

I liked Pancho. His gambling nature aside, I could relate to him.

He learned about tennis by running down balls at the Tennis Club of Guayaquil in Ecuador, where his father was a caretaker. Although he'd suffered from rickets as a child, which left him badly bow-legged, Segura developed a staggering two-fisted forehand and swung his way to tennis stardom — first as a player at the University of Miami, where he won the NCAA singles title three consecutive times during the 1940s, and later on the pro circuit alongside such notable players as Jack Kramer and Pancho Gonzalez. And playing credentials aside, Segura had built up quite a résumé as a coach. Among other feats, he'd guided his star pupil, Jimmy Connors, to victory at the Australian Open, Wimbledon, and the U.S. Open during the 1970s.

Despite his achievements, when Pancho offered to work with Andre, I turned him down. Back then, we had no idea what Andre's earning potential might be, but 12 percent sounded like one hell of a big chunk. Besides, I wasn't ready to let Andre go, to turn every aspect of his development as a player over to someone else. He was only 11, and he hadn't yet decided to stop listening to me.

That came later.

One evening, I saw a spot on *60 Minutes* called "Tennis Boot Camp" about a coach named Nick Bollettieri and the tennis academy he ran in Bradenton, Florida. I knew about Bollettieri, who, as the segment's title would suggest, was notorious for barking orders at players as he drilled them for hours at a stretch. A former paratrooper, Bollettieri ran a very strict program. Students of the academy lived in dorm rooms that could be described as Spartan at best, where they could expect random unannounced room checks;

drugs, alcohol, cigarettes, and junk food were prohibited. In the interest of fostering competition, kids were discouraged from becoming too friendly with each other; visiting in each other's rooms was not allowed. During the week, watching TV was forbidden, as were phone calls home. Those who did not obey Nick's code were subject to various punishments, from running laps to weeding Bollettieri's yard to waxing his car.

It wasn't Bollettieri's drill-sergeant persona that interested me, however. In fact, I wasn't really all that interested in Bollettieri at all. I'd met him before; he came through Vegas in the early 1960s when I was working at the Tropicana. He was friendly enough, but a little slick, a little phony for my taste. I could tell from that brief encounter that the guy didn't know jack about tennis. And by the time he'd founded the academy, he'd been married several times, which put me off. I know that doesn't have a thing to do with a guy's ability to coach, but I've always believed that marriage is a pretty sacred thing, so there you have it.

Rather, what interested me was that Bollettieri's academy boasted dozens of kids who played a mean game of tennis.

In Las Vegas, finding people for Andre to play with — to really challenge him — was next to impossible. All my kids were great players, but Andre in particular was simply in a class of his own. He was all over the court! Nobody who played him could figure out where he was going to hit the ball, and if they did, he hit it so damned hard they couldn't retrieve it anyway. He started playing tournaments at age eight, when he was just a little thing, and right from the start he beat 10-year-olds, 11-year-olds. Before he turned 10, he was beating all the 12-year-olds in our region and in California. By age 11, he was beating the 14-year-olds.

We used to drive all over Nevada, Utah, and California just to get Andre a decent game, and even then the pickings were slim. Adults didn't want to play him because it was embarrassing for them to lose (he was only in the eighth grade at the time), and there just weren't many kids his age around who held a candle to him.

That's not to say there was *no* competition. There was, for one, Pete Sampras, a gangly kid who was a year younger than Andre. But I'll be honest: Back when Andre and Pete played as juniors, I never thought Pete would turn into much of a player. In those days, he was pretty small and scrawny. His coach, Dr. Peter Fischer, used to put him in the 12-and-under division as a nine-year-old, and he'd get killed practically every time. Like Andre did back then, Pete played a serve-and-volley game, but because he was such a shrimp, his serve wasn't powerful enough to work to his advantage. Eventually, though, Pete's frame grew into his game; by the time he turned pro in 1988, Sampras stood 6′1″ and weighed in at 170 pounds. He was long-limbed and powerful, and the serve that had worked so poorly in the juniors had become as deadly as a guillotine and impossible to read.

In addition to meeting Sampras in the brackets, Andre frequently sparred with Michael Chang, another young Californian. Unlike Sampras, who flailed a bit in the juniors, Chang was always tough. Two years younger than Andre, he was as twitchy as a rabbit, and could run down just about anything you hit at him. Although Andre's age worked to his advantage against Chang in the juniors, enabling him to win more often than not, I suspected — correctly, as it turned out — that Chang would do well on the pro tour.

At Bollettieri's, though, there were any number of kids who could compete with Andre. They might not be quite as good, but they would at least challenge my son enough that he could continue to improve.

So one day, I called.

I'd gotten Nick's number a few months after that *60 Minutes* broadcast from a man whose own son, Aaron Krickstein, was a student at the academy. Dr. Krickstein had called me several times after watching Andre compete in Florida's Orange Bowl tournament. The Orange Bowl, an annual event, is known for drawing the best junior players from all over the globe, and is a very important tournament for young players who want to better their ranking.

According to Krickstein, Bollettieri had seen Andre play, and had dragged every pro he worked with and half his students along to observe. Hell, anytime Andre was on the docket, the stands surrounding other matches in play were so empty you half expected to see tumbleweeds float across the bleachers. At that time, Andre's game was completely different from anyone else's. He was so fast, hit the ball so early, hit it so freaking *hard*, it made it nearly impossible for anyone to return off of him. Nowadays, the whole world plays like that, but back then, it was new.

Bollettieri might not have known much about tennis, but even he could see that Andre was playing the game of the future. He wanted a piece of that action.

But when I finally called the academy, they played it cool and put me on hold. I waited, waited, waited for an eternity. I waited longer than I did to marry my wife. Finally, I got pissed off and hung up.

Five seconds later, the telephone rang and I picked it up.

"Mike!" said the voice on the other end.

"Yes," I answered.

"You hung up!"

"Yes," I said. "I'd waited long enough."

"Look, sorry about that. Let me go get Nick."

Suddenly, Bollettieri was on the phone.

"Hi Mike! Nick Bollettieri. Listen. I saw your son play. Helluva kid. I like him. I think I can help him."

"Okay," I said. We talked some more, and after settling on a reasonable fee, I agreed to send Andre on a trial basis for a month. So midway through the eighth grade, at the age of 13, Andre moved 3,000 miles away to Florida to attend school and train with Nick. He wasn't thrilled about leaving. He liked Las Vegas! He had friends here. But Andre also knew, even at that age, that if he played his cards right, if he stayed healthy and continued to develop, that one day he would make a lot of money playing tennis. A *lot* of money. And to a kid like Andre, that was compelling.

Not long after Andre arrived in Bradenton, several kids at the academy, including Andre, played in a tournament against some guys on a nearby college team. Andre drew the No. 2 seed, and took him in three sets. For a 13-year-old kid, taking out a college player got him fired up.

After the tournament, Nick called me. "That kid has the potential to be one of the greatest players of all time," he said. "I think he ought to stay."

I thought about it. I wasn't a rich man; by then, I was a show captain at the MGM Grand, and although the money was great by my standards, we certainly wouldn't have enough to survive *and* send Andre to the Nick Bollettieri Tennis Academy, which, in those days, ran about $20,000 a year. But I was determined to pay Andre's way, whatever it took. I knew it was the only way he could become a champion. I'd bet the house — mortgage it — if I had to.

"Let me talk to the boy," I said.

Nick put Andre on the phone. "Hi Dad," Andre said.

"Andre, what do you think? Do you want to stay?"

"I do," he said. "There are lots of great players here, and I'm learning a lot."

"Okay," I said. "Then stay. Put Nick on the phone."

As it turned out, my financial concerns were moot. Nick generously offered Andre a full scholarship.

Even though he'd agreed that staying at the academy was the best thing for him, life at Nick's was hard for Andre. He was homesick and lonely. He missed his friends in Las Vegas. Bollettieri was harsh, loud, and intimidating. The place was like an army camp. The students didn't have any freedom.

Predictably, Andre bucked like a rodeo steer under the academy's oppressive rules. One year, to vent his frustration, he destroyed dozens of Prince tennis rackets. He hurled them at the fences, lobbed them into the pool, smashed them on the court. Fortunately, by then, Prince was his sponsor, so the rackets were free; otherwise, I'm sure we would have had words. And although he was smart — Andre's one of the smartest guys I know — he didn't care much about academics, though he did manage to stay in school. He grew his hair long and dyed it, paying equal tribute to just about every shade in the rainbow. He wore makeup. Once, he wore a skirt in a tournament. He pierced his ears.

I'm a pretty traditional guy, yet all that stuff didn't bother me. Nick, however, was a different story. Andre's hooliganism drove his coach nuts. Once, after Andre played a tournament in jeans, Nick decided to humiliate Andre by chewing him out in front of the entire academy, which I thought was out of line. The way I saw it, you have to be realistic. I figured, when you're that good at something, you just don't give a damn what people think. Most geniuses are at least a little bit crazy, and as far as I was concerned, Andre was a genius. So for me, that battle just wasn't worth fighting.

I was, however, worried about Andre getting involved with drugs. I asked him if there were drugs around, and he said he didn't know, maybe there were, but he hadn't seen anything. Since he said "maybe," I thought there probably were. I voiced my fears to Nick, who wanted to use Andre as a stool pigeon; if Andre saw anyone with drugs, Nick wanted him to snitch. Andre declined.

To be fair, the academy might not have been totally to blame for Andre's misery. Part of it might have been general adolescent stuff — growing up, wanting to rebel.

Not long after Andre arrived, Nick offered Tami a scholarship as well, and we accepted. Even though I'd gone easy on her, Tami had developed into a fine player. I didn't think she'd wind up going pro, but I knew she was good enough to get a free ride playing tennis in college, which is exactly what she ended up doing after she graduated from Bollettieri's. In any case, for Tami, life at the academy was great. She likened it to being in a college dorm — if you could overlook (or skirt) the structure and rules. She loved meeting kids from all different backgrounds. She used to tease one kid because his dad's picture was on all the currency in his native country. There were too many rules, sure, but that didn't stop her from having fun.

And just as I'd thought, there were plenty of kids around to give Andre, and Tami, a good game. There was Andre's roommate Jim Courier, who, like Andre, would eventually claim the honor of a

No. 1 ranking. There were David Wheaton, whose ranking would peak at No. 12 in 1991, and Martin Blackman, who would compete on the tour for six years, claiming nine titles along the way. There was Mark Knowles, a Bahamian who would enjoy tremendous success as a doubles player. And of course, a few years ahead of him were Aaron Krickstein and Jimmy Arias, neither of whom would join that small fraternity of tennis legends, but who were damned fine players nonetheless.

Thanks in part to such tremendous competition at the academy, Andre's gift quickly shined through. In 1984, when he was 14, he won the National Boys Indoor 16-and-under singles and doubles championships. By age 15, he was considering turning pro.

There was just one problem: Bollettieri had, in my view, wrecked Andre's game. Andre went from a kid who played serve-and-volley tennis, who could nail every shot in the book, to a kid who camped out on the baseline. All the kids at Bollettieri's did! There they'd be, for hours at a time, slugging it out, never coming to the net, never mixing up their shots. Sure, they were hitting the snot out of the ball, but so what? They were so far away from the net, their opponent had plenty of time to scramble for the return. I mean, you half expected them to pitch a tent, stoke a fire, and start grilling s'mores back there.

I nearly lost my head.

Even though the prevailing wisdom had been to teach kids to be baseliners — indeed, most pros at the time ascribed to the theory — I'd deliberately taught Andre, taught *all* my kids, a serve-and-volley game. I knew that if tennis evolved the way I predicted it would, a serve-and-volley game would be more effective than a baseline approach. I felt that serve-and-volley players just had more complete games. Plus, it's much easier to put a point away at the net than it is from the baseline; otherwise, you run your butt off just to stay alive!

So I asked Nick, "What happened to Andre's net game?" And Nick replied, "What do you want? He's winning." I urged Nick to enter Andre into some doubles tournaments. I thought, if Andre plays doubles, he'll be forced to come to the net. He'll be forced to use a big serve, forced to volley. But Andre said he didn't want to, and Nick ignored my pleas.

He was in charge now. Who the hell was I?

I felt powerless.

As time passed, I grew more and more uncomfortable with the control Nick exercised over Andre. Once, I flew out to meet with a potential sponsor. While I was there, Andre played a match against a visiting top-ten French pro. The Frenchman had beaten all the other Bollettieri players, but hadn't played Andre yet. In the middle of the game, Andre mis-hit the ball and let fly a four-letter word. Nick heard it, and came after Andre, disciplining him like he was his own child. "You're not to use that kind of language!" he yelled. I agreed that Andre's behavior hadn't been appropriate, but it seemed odd to me that Nick would discipline him for it right in front of me when I hadn't said a word.

Later, after Andre won the match, we walked with Nick back to his office to meet with the sponsors. Andre turned to me and asked, "Dad, how did you like my game?"

"You played pretty good," I said. "You've improved."

This exchange apparently made Nick feel threatened, made him feel like his control over Andre was slipping, because he snapped. "I am the pro!" he said. "Not your dad! Anything you want to know, you ask me!"

Andre and I were stunned silent.

When we reached Nick's office, we found that the sponsor had not yet arrived, so I told Andre to wait outside. "I want to talk to Nick man to man," I said, and closed the door.

"Yes?" Nick said. "What's on your mind?"

"I'll tell you what's on my mind," I said. "Always be afraid of what people say behind you, not in front of you."

Nick waited for me to continue.

"If Andre asks me a question behind your back and I give him an answer you don't agree with, then you're in trouble. But if he asks me a question right in front of you, it means he *respects* you. He knows you are his coach. He's not going behind your back! He just wanted to know what I thought."

Nick sighed. "You're right," he said. "I'm sorry. I was wrong."

I said, "Don't tell *me* you were wrong. It doesn't matter to me. You have to tell the kid."

But he wouldn't. "I'm not going to apologize to him," he said. He didn't want to lose face with Andre.

Incredibly, in spite of behavior like this, Bollettieri still managed to win the battle for Andre's heart and mind. Nick was no idiot. Kids like Andre were Nick's bread and butter. Nick knew that Andre was the real deal, that Andre's career was about to take off like the space shuttle, and he intended to be along for the ride. Once Nick figured out just how talented Andre was, he was forever hanging out with Andre, taking him out to eat, out to the movies. I even began to suspect that Nick wanted Andre to fall in love with one of his daughters, just to keep him in the family. I don't know if that's true — maybe I'm just being paranoid — but it did cross my mind.

With Andre, I had two jobs: coach and father, and both were equally important. In addition to teaching Andre to play, I needed to teach him to be a decent human being. Bollettieri, on the other hand, had only one job: coach. That left him free to pal around with Andre off the court. What kid *wouldn't* prefer fun over discipline?

But in the end, all the movies and steak dinners in the world weren't enough to keep Andre in Bradenton. Bottom line, the kid was unhappy. He never really made any friends at Nick's academy because, well, Nick didn't want him to. Eventually, Andre grew *so* unhappy that he threatened to leave. To appease Andre, Nick suggested we send Phillip to live with him at the academy. By then, Phillip had left UNLV after two years of studies and had spent a few years on the satellite circuit, but he was ready to move on to something different. He knew that Andre was going to make it big, that Andre would need his help, and he was happy to give it. Just as my older brother Sam had looked after me when I first moved to America, Phillip would look after Andre.

You know, I made a lot of sacrifices for Andre over the years — teaching him to play, driving him to matches — but I'd say that before it was all over, Phillip, who would travel with Andre for the better part of a decade on the tour circuit after keeping him company in Bradenton, made even more.

And it was a good thing, too, because if Phillip hadn't gone to Florida, I would have had to quit my job and move down there myself. That would have been a huge gamble! Andre would have had to earn enough money to support the whole family, which would have put him under a lot of pressure. I did everything I could to avoid that.

But for Andre, the pressure came anyway.

CHAPTER EIGHT

"If my career was over tomorrow, I had a lot more than I deserved."
— Andre Agassi, after winning Wimbledon in 1992

Here's how things happen for most tennis legends: First they become great, then they become famous, and *then* they become rich.

For Andre, it was the exact opposite.

In Andre's case, the money came first, lots of it. Long before Andre proved himself on the court — hell, long before he was even old enough to *vote* — he began raking in high-dollar endorsement deals. There was Nike; Canon; a watch deal; those hideous denim tennis shorts; Prince rackets, and later, Donnay.

The fame came next. Here he was, this MTV kid with a crushing forehand who had long crazy hair, and who was dressed like a homeless skateboarder who had just robbed a jewelry store. In a lineup of tennis pros, Andre stood out like a feather boa on a stockbroker. And it wasn't just his looks, his clothes; it was his personality, his instinctive ability to enjoy himself on the court, his propensity to fool around. After a decade of Lendl's and Borg's robotic demeanor, of McEnroe's petulant outbursts, of Connors's charismatic antagonism,

Andre's Elvis-like showmanship was, for many, as refreshing as a breeze in the desert.

For Andre, tennis was a show. It was about pleasing the audience. They paid to see him, and he made sure they got their money's worth. It wasn't important to him to win. If it had been, he would have.

Which is why greatness didn't come until later.

Much later.

In 1986, the year Andre went pro, life for Betty and me was much like it always was. We went to work. We came home. We had our own lives to lead, and we led them. Instead of traveling the circuit with Andre, we tapped Phillip to chaperone. To keep abreast of things, we watched matches on TV or read the results in the paper. In short, we let him go, just the way my parents had let me go when I moved to America.

It was difficult for Betty, especially since Andre was the baby of the family, but not for me.

To be honest, I don't know how any parent can stand to travel the tour. Calling the tour a grind is like calling the desert a sand trap: a gross understatement, especially when you're traveling with a kid who's still struggling to make it. Andre's early years on the tour didn't involve a private jet, limos, and hotel suites. Rather, it involved flying coach, catching a courtesy shuttle, and hunkering down in a room in some two-star chain hotel — for 40 weeks a year. That's because unlike soccer, baseball, basketball, football, hockey, rugby, auto racing, or even bowling, tennis doesn't have a season — which means, by extension, that it doesn't have an *off* season. Sure, there's a month or so before Christmas when the schedule gets pretty thin, but that's about it. The rest of the time, you're on the road. Compare that to the NFL schedule: The regular season starts in late August and lasts until early December. If a team makes the playoffs, the season gets stretched until late January or early February at the latest. They play one game a week, and 50 percent of all games are at home, which means the guys aren't traveling anywhere near as much as a tennis pro like Andre does.

No thanks. I could do without the constant travel.

In any case, I suspect that Andre was grateful for our distance. You show me a 16-year-old who wants to hang out with his parents all the time and I'll show you one maladjusted kid. Besides, there wasn't anything I could teach him by then that he didn't already know — about tennis or about life. Even if there had been, I doubt he would have listened.

By then, Andre had plenty of other people watching out for him. There was Nick, for one. Although Andre had been miserable at Bollettieri's academy, he'd enlisted Nick as his primary coach, probably out of a sense of loyalty. Incidentally, Andre was about the only player who kept Nick around after turning pro. Arias dumped him. Krickstein dumped him. Courier dumped him. Seles dumped him. Nobody stayed! But Andre is the type of guy that if you're nice to him, he cannot turn against you. He didn't want to hurt Nick. Andre also had an agent, Bill Shelton, who was a friend of Nick's, and had a hitting partner and a ball feeder. And there was Phillip, of course. "Team Agassi," they called themselves.

I was not a member, and in all candor, I was fine with that.

I didn't much care who Andre tapped for advice or who got the credit as long as he was successful. For me, it was like that story of

King Solomon and the two mothers. The story goes that a woman wakes up in the middle of the night to discover that her newborn baby has died. Crazy with grief, she switches her dead baby with the live one at another woman's breast, but denies it when the duped woman wakes up. To settle the dispute, the women request an audience with King Solomon, who proposes to resolve the issue by sawing the live baby in two, giving half to one mother and half to the other. Horrified, the child's true mother begs the king to spare the infant even if it means awarding the other woman custody, while the impostor demands that the child be divided. In this way, King Solomon determines the child's true mother, noting "She loves her son so much, she is willing to give him to another so that he may live."

That's how I felt about Andre.

It sounds sort of heavy-handed, but for me, the most important thing — the *only* thing — was Andre reaching his potential. If that meant keeping my distance, turning him over to the care of others, letting others claim the credit, then so be it.

In 1986, Andre earned a whopping $22,574 in tournament winnings. He raked in more than most American 16-year-olds, but then again, most American 16-year-olds don't have a staff to support. Although he reached the finals in Schenectady, New York, and the semis at Stratton Mountain, Vermont (where, as a wildcard entry, he lost to John McEnroe), and although he whittled his ranking from No. 603 to No. 100, ending the year at No. 102, Andre's arrival on the scene made barely a ripple in the ATP pond.

The next year was better, although he did get humiliated at

Wimbledon, losing in straight sets in the first round to Henri Leconte. (Leconte had Andre's number, apparently; he beat my boy again that year at the U.S. Open, though this time, Andre did manage to lasso a set.) In fact, Andre had such a bad time at the All England Lawn Tennis & Croquet Club he skipped Wimbledon the next three years. "I'm not ready," he said one year. "I need rest," he said the next. Martina Navratilova's response to Andre's decision summed up the feelings of many, including mine, when she said that a tennis player skipping Wimbledon to rest is "like a football player who skips the Super Bowl because he has to get ready for training camp." But it wasn't important to him. He hated the grass, which dies after the first round anyway; hated the dress code; hated that it took the All England Club 40 years to switch from using a white ball to using a yellow ball. He just didn't like playing there.

But that year Andre *did* reach the quarters in Tokyo and Los Angeles. At Stratton Mountain, after ousting reigning Wimbledon champ Pat Cash in the second round, Andre tore headway through his bracket to meet Ivan Lendl in the semis. Lendl beat Andre so badly in the first set, 6–2, you half expected him to punctuate the win by stealing Andre's lunch money afterward. Andre rallied and managed to win the second set 7–5, but was broken twice in the third and lost the match as a result. Despite the loss, his run at Stratton gave him confidence; and later that year, in Brazil, Andre won the first ATP title of his career. By the end of 1987, during which he won $163,511 in prize money, he'd boosted his ranking to No. 41 in the world.

When Andre went pro at 16, the guy that managed his sponsors and his schedule claimed huge chunks of his income, and the contract, as thick as a phone book, was steeped with clauses. From what I understood of the contract, it seemed like the manager could earn a dollar each time Andre even *thought* about tennis. But by the end of 1987, I figured we were in a position to negotiate. And because Andre was still a minor, and because Betty and I were still his legal guardians, that meant I'd be the one to do the talking.

"You get 10 percent of endorsements and 15 percent of tournament winnings," I told the agent. "Not 20 and 25. And that's only if you put Andre in the tournament yourself. If a tournament director contacts Andre directly and Andre ends up playing in the tournament, he doesn't owe you a dime. Moreover, I don't want an earnings minimum. I don't want to put Andre under that kind of pressure."

"We can't do that," he said.

I said, "Then forget it."

"You're never going to find anyone else to do that, either."

"Then we'll get a lawyer and go it alone."

"You'll ruin his life," he warned.

"Fine," I said. "Then *I'll* ruin his life. I'm not going to let *you* do it."

So I got a lawyer, and we drafted a one-page contract. It was so simple, any sixth-grader could read it and understand it. To give the agent one more chance, I sent it to him. I said, "If you want it, sign it. Otherwise, don't call me anymore."

In response, he drew up a new contract and sent it to me. "It's exactly like yours," he said.

"If it's exactly like mine, then sign *mine*."

No go. So I picked up the phone and called Bob Kane at IMG, a management group that also happened to own Bollettieri's academy.

"I've written a contract for my son," I said. "If you want to accept it, then sign. If not, then I'm signing with my lawyer, and we'll go that way." Already, every tournament was clamoring for Andre; wherever he went, it sold out. We'd do just fine.

"Let me take a look at it," he said. Five hours later, he was on a plane. We went out to dinner, I talked, and he listened. Afterward, at our house, I handed him the contract, and he signed it in a heartbeat. I don't even think he bothered to read it.

"How much money do you think my son is going to make this year?" I asked afterward.

"I don't know," he answered. "Five-, six-, seven-hundred-thousand dollars?"

"What if I told you he'll make between two and three million dollars? What would you say?"

"I'd say this will end up being the best deal I've made for this company in a while," he answered.

That year, my son signed with several sponsors, including Nike, Canon cameras, and a watch company. His career was going in every direction. *Every* direction.

He made more than $2 million.

In 1988, the year he turned 18, Andre's star officially rose. He earned more than half a million dollars in prize money and peaked at No. 3 in the world. In addition to winning titles in Memphis, Charleston, Forest Hills, Stuttgart, Stratton Mountain, and Livingston, Andre made it to the quarters in Orlando, Rome, and Boston; to the semis at Indian Wells and the French Open, losing to Boris Becker and Mats Wilander, respectively; and to the finals in Los Angeles.

He had become a star.

However, 1989 was a different story. Andre managed to stay in the top ten — in fact, all told, his ranking slipped just a few slots to No. 7 — but he claimed only a single title, in Orlando. And as soon as he slipped, the whispers began — especially when Andre lost in the third round of the 1989 French Open to Jim Courier, his former bunkmate at Bollettieri's, who Andre had ripped to pieces on countless occasions. Maybe Andre wasn't tennis's second coming after all, they said. Maybe he really *was* just "Wayne Newton in denim," as reporter Curry Kirkpatrick so bluntly wrote in *Sports Illustrated*. And when Andre's old foe on the California courts, 17-year-old Michael Chang, took the French Open title that year at Roland Garros, it was almost like Andre became an afterthought.

As for me, I knew Andre had what it took to make it. But I also knew he just didn't care. He didn't apply himself. I could see it. My guess is he was just making too much money. If he won, his contracts didn't get better, so why bother? Even so, things improved in 1990. Andre won in San Francisco, Key Biscayne, and Washington, D.C., and claimed the Singles Championship title in Germany, but lost in the finals at Indian Wells, Roland Garros, and the U.S. Open. So even though Andre had again risen in the rankings, the whispers continued — especially after the French, which he'd been heavily favored to win, but which he lost to 30-year-old Andres Gomez. Then, another blow: The gangly serve-and-volleyer Pete Sampras, who in the juniors could barely give Andre a game, crushed Andre in the finals at Flushing Meadows to claim the U.S. Open title — in straight sets no less.

There it was: My proof that Nick shouldn't have morphed Andre from a serve-and-volley player into a baseliner. Andre might not have won that match as a serve-and-volleyer, but surely he'd have won at least a set.

In 1991, Andre again reached the finals at the French Open, and again suffered a painful loss, losing to Courier. Again he'd been favoured to win, and again he blew it.

Chang. Sampras. Courier. All players Andre had dominated in his youth. Yet all three had beaten Andre to a Grand Slam title.

The same year, Andre finally took another stab at Wimbledon, but lost in the quarters to David Wheaton. The whispers got louder. Five years he'd been on the tour, and still no major! And when Aaron Krickstein ejected Andre from the U.S. Open in the first round, things just got worse.

After Andre's loss to Krickstein, I ran into Nick at the stadium.

"Well," he said. "What do you think?"

"I'll tell you something," I said. "If it were me, I'd have Andre practice two against one. If he can make points against two people, he can make points against one anytime. Second, I'd get Rod Laver to be his second coach."

Nick puffed up. "He doesn't need a coach! I am the coach. Besides, Laver plays an old man's game."

Whatever. Laver had coached Sampras for a time, after all. One thing was for sure: Laver knew a hell of a lot more about the game than Nick did.

"Well, you asked," I said. "And I'm telling you."

Andre began to doubt himself. "The pessimistic side of me questions if I'll ever win one," he told reporters after losing the French. You could see it in the perpetually panicky expression on his face: His confidence plummeted. He started to second-guess himself. His strokes became tentative.

Some attributed his failures to fitness and preparation — or more precisely, lack thereof. I concede that Andre wasn't known for eating properly. This was a kid who dined at McDonald's every night during the 1988 French Open. Before he got his own plane, he used to call the airlines ahead of time and order cheeseburgers for his flights. He contended that cheeseburgers with the works contained your four basic food groups, and therefore, despite the fat, cholesterol, calories, and God knows what else, qualified as "healthy." If he couldn't find food he liked at a tournament locale, he'd eat candy — big bags of Reese's and Snickers.

I'll even concede that Andre might not have been in the greatest condition back in those days. He had a trainer — he'd hired Gil Reyes, a strength and conditioning coach at UNLV, in 1989 — but I can't say he always took Gil's advice to heart back then the way he does now. Over the years, Andre came to like and trust Gil so much that he not only kept him as his trainer, he named his first-born child, Jaden Gil Agassi, after him.

But the preparation issue? That's another thing entirely. For most players, preparation begins weeks before a tournament. But for Andre, things are different. Let's assume today is Saturday, and that his first match in a tournament is on Tuesday. That means he'll practice 30 minutes on Sunday, an hour on Monday, 15 minutes on Tuesday, and then go play his match. He could practice longer, but why? He has hit so many million balls, he doesn't need to.

Nonetheless, Andre began to listen to these whispers. He went on a low-fat diet. He began logging insane hours on the practice court. Neither helped. The ceaseless practice made him too tired come match time, and the diet caused cramping. As 1991 folded into 1992, desperate, Andre experimented with his strings, his serve, his footwork, but quickly gave up and changed them all back.

By May of 1992, he'd tumbled out of the top ten for the first time since 1988. "My ranking deserves to be slipping," Andre told *Sports Illustrated*. "And it may not stop here."

When Wimbledon rolled around in 1992, I can't say I expected much. Andre's ranking had continued to plummet; coming into the tournament, he was No. 17 in the world. But of course I watched. In the first round, I watched him drop the first set against Andrei Chesnokov, but then charge back to take the next three sets. The same in round two against Eduardo Masso. I watched him straight-set Derrick Rostagno and Christian Saceanu in rounds three and four, respectively. I watched him take Becker in the five-set quarterfinal, and I watched him demolish an aging — but still entertaining — McEnroe in the semis, three sets to nil.

And on the day of the finals, against Goran Ivanisevic, Betty and I watched my son's destiny press forward to meet him. Our Andre, who'd so painfully thrown away three chances for a Grand Slam title during a career so bumpy he should have signed on to endorse Dramamine, kept his head even as Ivanisevic zinged ace after ace — 37 in all. He kept his head after losing the first set in a tiebreak, after breaking Goran twice to win the second and third sets, even after losing in the fourth. He kept his head in the fifth when, down a break point, he held serve.

In the final game of the match, it was Goran, not Andre, who began to crumble. Goran double-faulted twice before fighting to tie things up 30 all. After Andre managed a forehand pass off a weak volley, it was match point.

I sat up in my chair. "Come on," I said more to myself than to Betty. "Come *on!*"

Ivanisevic tossed, swung. Nothing but net. Fault.

I exhaled, inhaled, exhaled again. Goran bounced the ball a few times, and then launched his second serve.

Andre: A backhand return.

Goran: A backhand volley. Again, into the net.

Andre had done it. He had won! As he fell to the turf, weeping, Betty and I leaped from our seats, screaming.

"He won!" she yelled.

"He did it!" I hollered.

We'd done it.

In the autumn of 1992, after Wimbledon, Andre sat me down in the living room for a talk. He was 22.

"Dad," he said, "I need a break."

"Okay," I said.

He continued. "It's just, I never had a childhood. I never had a girlfriend. I never had a prom. I feel like I missed out on so much."

I disputed the girlfriend part. By then, there had been one or two. But otherwise, he was right. He had missed out on a lot. I'd always been strict with Andre. From the very beginning, I knew Andre could be one of the greatest players of all time. I also knew if he got hurt along the way, he could jeopardize his whole future. That meant when his friends went skiing, skateboarding, or rock climbing, or did any other activity that might end with a broken shoulder or a blown knee, Andre stayed home. I'd pounded that into his head — especially after his mother took him ice skating when he was 10, a day that ended with Andre in the hospital. He'd fallen down, and somebody had skated over his fingers.

"I think I want to take some time, just relax, enjoy myself. Then I'll be ready to come back, ready to work."

"Take your time," I said. "When you want to be No. 1, be No. 1." He nodded.

"But let me give you some facts of life," I said. "Right now, everybody is at this level." I saluted in front of my eyes to signal height. "Two years from now," I continued, raising my hand above my head, "everybody is going to be at *this* level. It won't be as easy to win the tournaments you're winning now in two, three years."

"You're right," he said.

"If you want to wait, that's fine. But when you come back, winning is going to be far more difficult, because today's players are much better than yesterday's players, and they're getting better."

So I wasn't that surprised when Andre tanked a bit in 1993. He continued to play, and even won a few tournaments, but he just didn't put much into it. He hung out with his friends, tinkered with his cars. He bought a plane. As usual, he skipped the Australian Open, this time citing bronchitis, and bailed on Roland Garros because of tendonitis in his wrist. His ranking fell sharply, bottoming out at No. 31 before easing back into the top 20.

Bollettieri, on the other hand, was pissed.

He was pissed that Andre wasn't particularly interested in training. He was upset by Andre's double-chin and belly, which had developed after months of relative inactivity, even though Gil Reyes blamed the bloating on the cortisone shots that had been injected into Andre's wrist.

He was angry, too, that Andre had sought guidance on his game from others, including tennis greats John McEnroe and Pancho Segura. Nick felt threatened. He knew that if Andre drifted from his control, his career as Andre's coach might well end, which some might interpret as a mark on his reputation, not to mention the academy's. The fact was, as each year on the tour with Andre passed, Bollettieri had reaped the rewards of my son's success; enrollment at the Bradenton academy multiplied, no doubt in part because of the substantial publicity Andre's success generated. Certainly, the banner he strung from the rafters of the academy's gymnasium that read "Andre Agassi, Wimbledon Champion, 1992" became a powerful draw.

But most of all, Nick was angry because, inexplicably, he believed, as he wrote it in his book *My Aces My Faults*, "that [he] had been generous, even lavish, in [his] dealings with Andre, and [he] didn't feel [Andre] had quite reciprocated." Specifically, Nick estimated that he and the academy had invested at least $1 million to develop Andre's talent, what with coaching, rooms, board, travel, hitting partners, and the like. In return, however, he and the academy had received less than $400,000 — though he did concede that his association with Andre had yielded "substantial publicity."

Who knows what the numbers were; I never saw the books. But I do know that Andre gave Nick plenty, maybe even more than he deserved. Even before Andre had started earning serious money, he bought Nick a Corvette. Early in Andre's career, Nick talked him into shooting a video for the camp; Andre was supposed to get a commission, but never got a dime. And there is no doubt that the "substantial publicity" Nick mentioned had been worth an astronomical amount. If it hadn't been for Andre, I bet that academy would have closed years ago. But thanks in large part to my son, kids still come from all over the world to train with Bollettieri. Besides, Nick was never on our payroll; he was on International Management Group's. IMG had bought the academy in 1984, and Nick was *their* employee, not ours.

In any case, after 10 years as Andre's coach, Nick abruptly resigned shortly after Wimbledon in 1993. Instead of informing Andre of his decision in person, however, Bollettieri sent him a letter — but leaked the news to a reporter before Andre got a chance to read it.

Andre was devastated.

It wasn't so much that Andre wanted Nick to continue as his coach; he didn't. Andre and I had even talked about cutting Nick loose and finding someone else. But Andre was loyal; he never wanted to stab Nick in the back. So even though Andre wasn't wild about how things were going with Nick, it still hurt when Nick severed the tie. It's like a bad marriage: Just because you're unhappy with your wife doesn't mean it doesn't hurt when she tells you she's leaving.

Nick and Andre's breakup was ugly. After Nick left, Andre told reporters that Nick had been "insignificant" to his career, though I suspect he later regretted the comment. Months later, Andre reached out to Nick to clear the air, but Nick only continued his campaign for compensation, first cornering Andre's business manager, Perry Rogers, and later penning a letter directly to Andre spelling out his case. Simply put, Nick was willing to continue his relationship with Andre, but only for a price — odd for a man who frequently claimed that money wasn't important to him. According to Nick, he'd given up his family for Andre; his fifth wife had issued an ultimatum, "It's Andre or us," and he'd chosen

Andre. Nick had, in turn, given up Andre for money — or at least that's the way Andre saw it. "Bollettieri," Andre told *Tennis* magazine, "is absolutely disrespectful, has no integrity, has no class, and quite honestly, if everyone in the world was like him, it would absolutely be a horrible place to live."

I would never wish unhappiness upon my son, but I can't say I was entirely sorry to see Nick go. He built an empire on my son's back, and nearly destroyed him in the process. Wounded by Nick's departure, Andre fell into a terrible funk. He was eliminated in the first round of the U.S. Open, and did not play again for the rest of the year. Painful scar tissue in his wrist, the one that performed the snap I'd taught him in order to generate more torque in his forehand, demanded surgery in December. Adrift and alone, Andre's rank plummeted as his weight ballooned; he finished the year ranked No. 24, and tipped the scales more than 15 pounds above his fighting weight.

And, from my perspective anyway, things were about to get worse.

Andre, 1st Good Shepherd School,
Las Vegas, 1976

Young Andre Agassi

Andre at soccer practice,
Las Vegas, 1978

Andre (second from right) and Ty Tucker, Jr. Doubles Tournament

Andre on backyard court
at Tara house, 1984

Pancho Gonzalez, Rita Agassi Gonzalez, and Phillip Agassi at Carnation Tournament, Hawaii, 1985

Andre, Nick Bollettieri camp, 1985

Andre at Indianapolis, 1987

Andre, Hamlet Tournament, 1988

Andre, Stratton Mountain Tournament, 1989

Pancho Gonzalez
and son Skylar,
1991

Pancho Gonzalez
and Skylar, Las
Vegas, 1992

Andre catches up on news from home

Hanging with the boys. Mike with Andre and Phillip, 1992.

Mike Agassi practices on home court, 1994

Mike and Betty with their U.S. Open champion, 1994

Andre with sisters Rita and Tami and brother Phillip, 1994

Mike and Betty attend the U.S. Open, 1995

Phillip's wedding, San Diego, 1995. (L-R): Tami, Andre, Mike, Marti, Phillip, Rita, Betty, and Skylar

Mike, Marti, Phillip, and Betty, 1995

Brooke Shields, Mike, Betty, and Andre at Phillip's wedding, 1995

Andre, goofing around with Skylar, with Mom and Dad, 1995

Andre and Brooke Shields (Mike in background), Idaho, Christmas 1997

Just another day on the job. Mike and members of KISS at MGM, 1999.

Mike with boxer Roy Jones, Jr. at MGM Grand, Las Vegas, 2000

Martina Navratilova, Tami Agassi, and Mike at a cancer fundraiser in Seattle, 2001

Andre, Mike, and Jim Courier at a cancer function in Seattle, 2001

Back row: Mona and Jack Ratelle (Phillip's in-laws), Heidi Graff, and Jaden.
Front row: Marti, Carter, Phillip, Mike, Betty, Steffi, and Andre, 2002

Mike with grandson Jaden, 2003

Jaden and Jaz Agassi, Christmas 2003

Mike Agassi

CHAPTER NINE

"We're so in tune, it's surreal."

— Brooke Shields

Women practically threw themselves at Andre from the moment he joined the tour; as Nick once famously noted, even old ladies at Wimbledon liked him. But despite plenty of opportunities, by the time he was 24 years old, Andre had been interested in only three women in his life: Amy Moss, a member of the hospitality team at a tournament in Memphis; Wendi Stewart, a neighbor of ours on Tara Street in Las Vegas who, for a time, traveled with Andre on the tour; and Barbra Streisand, who . . . well, you all know who *she* is. For the record, as far as I know anyway, Barbra and Andre really were just good friends.

And then he met Brooke Shields.

Brooke, then 29, had quite a story of her own. Brooke's parents divorced shortly after she was born, and Brooke's mother, Teri, a former model, was awarded custody. Teri, sensing the infant Brooke's appeal, launched her daughter into the spotlight before Brooke could even walk, and her efforts paid off quickly. At two, Brooke became the Ivory Snow girl.

Not that I can talk, what with my training Andre to follow a tennis ball with his eyes from the moment he was bundled home from the hospital, but Teri's overzealousness with Brooke's career unnerved even *me*. Determined to see her daughter succeed, Teri chose roles for Brooke that were guaranteed to generate publicity. Brooke was the 12-year-old prostitute in *Pretty Baby*, the sloe-eyed 15-year-old tease who, wearing a pair of Calvin Klein jeans and not much else, breathily posed the question on everyone's minds: "You know what comes between me and my Calvins?" And of course, there was *Blue Lagoon*, the movie in which a young Brooke spent the better portion of her screen time topless. Even so, Brooke and her mother invested a lot of energy insisting that Brooke was a virgin (had anyone even asked?), not unlike the beautiful Russian tennis player, Anna Kournikova, would years later.

Although Brooke remained a paparazzi darling, her career flagged during her 20s, during which Brooke's work opportunities were essentially limited to drippy movie-of-the-week roles and endorsement gigs in Japan, with the occasional game-show guest spot. In the meantime, she was connected to a bizarre slew of men, including George Michael, Liam Neeson, Michael Bolton, Dean Cain, John Kennedy, Jr., Dodi Al-Fayed, the Crown Prince of Japan, and, of course, Michael Jackson. (Brooke insisted that her relationship with Jacko was platonic.)

Even so, she wasn't as flashy as many Hollywood types. She was sweet natured, well mannered, reserved, sensitive, and rather bright — she had attended Princeton during a hiatus from acting. And despite the critical drubbing she often received, she did take her work seriously. Those were qualities that Andre could appreciate.

Set up by a mutual friend, Lyndie Benson, wife of saxophonist Kenny G., Andre and Brooke were, in certain respects, well matched.

Brooke even had tennis connections: In the "It's a Small World" category, Brooke's grandfather, Frank Shields, had played on the victorious American Davis Cup team in 1933, and had been friendly with Pancho Gonzalez; the two played the occasional doubles match together.

Both Andre and Brooke are very spiritual people. Both were child prodigies. Both were powerfully motivated — some would say browbeaten — by their parents to succeed, Brooke by her mother and Andre by me. Both had high-profile careers, ones that had experienced serious bumps over the years. Those high-profile careers, however, limited their time together; Andre was a slave to the tour, and Brooke had movies — mainly of the direct-to-video variety — to shoot. They courted each other by fax for months before officially going out in December of 1993.

As nice as Brooke seemed, I had serious reservations about the relationship from the very beginning. Of course, the media frenzy their union had spawned concerned me. When their relationship became public, even Andre, hardly a stranger to the press, was stunned by the circus that followed Brooke's every move. Any time Brooke was in the stands while Andre played a match, the camera focused on her at least as much as it focused on him. It wasn't so much that Andre resented the shift of attention away from him, although I suspect he wasn't wild about the idea; rather, the whole thing was just so *distracting*.

Even though Andre had decided beforehand to take it easy in 1993, it had wound up being a lousy year. He'd been left by Bollettieri. He'd endured a string of bitter losses. He dropped to

No. 24 in the rankings and ended the year laid up and overweight after wrist surgery. If he intended to stage a comeback after his layoff like we'd talked about, the absolute last thing he needed was to be distracted.

Besides, I wasn't particularly impressed with Hollywood types generally. Their track record with relationships didn't exactly inspire confidence. It just seems like most of them don't believe in pure love, pure life, one marriage. Read the stories: Zsa Zsa Gabor, married eight times; Elizabeth Taylor, married eight times; Frank Sinatra, married four times. They don't say "I do" forever; they say "I do" until tomorrow.

In fact, I was *so* worried, that when Andre brought Brooke home to meet us, I blurted out "I hope you two aren't planning to get married!" I knew it couldn't work, couldn't last.

In retrospect, that didn't do much to foster closeness with my son.

In 1994, Andre proved my fears — about his game, anyway — unfounded. After five months away from the tour, during which he'd done some hard thinking about his future, he blazed back. In February, he won a tournament in Scottsdale. In March, he reached the finals of the Lipton Championships in Key Biscayne after besting Boris Becker, Cedric Pioline, Stefan Edberg, and Patrick Rafter, falling finally to Pete Sampras. Andre showcased his class at Key Biscayne when, on the morning of the final, Sampras woke up feeling nauseated. Rather than accepting a victory by default, Andre agreed to delay the match's start until after Sampras could be treated by a physician.

As 1994 progressed, Andre's winning ways continued. He advanced to the fourth round at Wimbledon. He won the U.S. Open — his second career Grand Slam trophy — for the first time, defeating Michael Stich in straight sets to become the first unseeded player to claim the title since 1966. It was powerful stuff. He was focused and fierce and determined, savvy and poised, and it paid off. As Andre served out the last game of the third set in Flushing Meadows, Betty and I were beside ourselves with pride.

By the end of the year, Andre had beaten every player in the top ten and clawed his way back to No. 2 in the world. Not content, he won the Australian Open in early 1995, defeating Pete Sampras in the final. It was an emotional match. Sampras, distraught over the recent collapse of his coach, Tim Gullikson — who was later diagnosed with brain cancer and tragically passed away in May of 1996 at age 44 — came out with guns blazing in the first set, winning it 6–4. But Andre kept his composure and slugged his way back into the match, winning the next three sets to claim the title.

For Andre, the 1995 Australian Open title was the first of many in Melbourne; he'd go on to bag the crown there in 2000, 2001, and 2003. But frankly, Andre's mere *attendance* at the Australian Open, a tournament he'd declined to play in the past because it was "too far away from home," despite the fact that it was one of only four Grand Slams on the tour calendar, signaled to me that Andre had rededicated himself to the game. The wins were just gravy.

In April of 1995, amidst a 26-match winning streak, Andre squeaked into the No. 1 spot for the first time in his career. Even better, thanks at least in part to Brooke's influence, he drastically improved his training regimen and eating habits. By clocking in two and a half hours of gym time a day (he could bench press nearly 300 pounds!) and eschewing Taco Bell and Big Gulps, Andre shed the weight he'd gained in the fall of 1993 and then some.

Perhaps most amazing of all, he cut his hair off. In one swift motion, the over-processed rat's nest that had come to symbolize Andre's flash, his flamboyance, was gone. He'd started balding anyway, so he decided it was time to bite the bullet.

Things were good for Brooke, too. With Andre's support, she fired her mother as manager and signed on with Perry Rogers, who in addition to being Andre's business manager was also his childhood friend. She was quickly rewarded. In the fall of 1994, Brooke joined the cast of the Broadway production of *Grease*; that autumn, Andre spent more time backstage than he did on court. In 1995, she landed a guest spot on the hit show *Friends* that showcased her comedic talents; that led to the creation of Brooke's own NBC sitcom, *Suddenly Susan*, in 1996. Slotted between *Seinfeld* and *ER*, *Suddenly Susan* couldn't fail.

Although Andre credited Brooke with his about-face in life ("She's turned my life around," he told *People* magazine), Brad Gilbert got the recognition for Andre's return to form on the court. Andre had hired Brad, himself a former player on the tour, in the spring of 1994.

I'll be honest: I've never been able to figure out just what a coach can do for a top-ten player. A coach's basic duty is to assess his students' weaknesses and to work on them, but what can you teach a guy who already knows everything about the game? Besides, Rod Laver never had a coach. Pancho Gonzalez never had a coach. Arthur Ashe never had a coach. Roger Federer dumped his coach in late 2003, but that didn't stop him from reclaiming the No. 1 spot in early 2004. Sure, a coach will scout other players for you, but couldn't you go watch them yourself? And in the end, how much can a coach really be trusted? Your coach is not your family. He's there to make a living.

But okay, I'll admit that signing on with Brad was a good idea. I swear the guy has a photographic memory. You can ask him about a match seven years ago, and he can recount every point. When it comes to scouting other players, Brad's the man. He did a good job preparing Andre for his opponents.

Plus, Andre's one weakness — his mental game — was Brad's strength. Brad had even written a book called *Winning Ugly,* which teaches readers how to gain that critical mental edge over their opponents, an edge he'd enjoyed against Andre in four out of the eight matches they played during Brad's pro career. As Andre put it, "He has spent his whole career winning matches he shouldn't have won. I've done the opposite: I've lost a lot of matches I shouldn't have lost."

Fortunately, Brad wasn't afraid to point out Andre's weaknesses. And because Brad had faced many of the opponents that Andre encountered, he had, in Andre's eyes, a bit more credibility than, say, Bollettieri or, say, me. Besides, they were friends, they liked each other. What more could you want from a guy who's going to spend every waking moment with you? Andre did say things might be better if Brad talked less, but he was smiling when he said it.

But I was disappointed, too, because I'd hoped that Brad would be more open to my suggestions than Nick had been. Take Andre's strings: I have long believed that he uses the wrong kind. He uses Kevlar strings, and they make the racket so hard, it's like a board!

Nobody plays like that but him. So I suggested to Brad that they fiddle with Andre's strings, and maybe lengthen the handle a bit to amp up Andre's serve and strokes. No go. Maybe Brad was afraid that if he took my advice and it worked, Andre might decide to fire him and hire someone else.

Another time, I took Brad aside. "I'm going to tell you something you might not know," I said.

"Hmm," he replied.

"All the big servers," I named 10 names. "What do they have in common?"

"They're all tall?" Brad said.

"Yes, they're all tall," I replied. "And?"

"And . . . they're all strong?"

"Yeah, they're all tall, they're all strong. They all eat food! But what do they have in common? Why does Sampras have a big serve?"

"You tell me," he said.

"*They all play with a mid-sized racket,*" I said. "It goes through the air faster than an oversized racket! It's simple physics! Even a blind man can see that. Plus, if you get a longer handle, you generate even more power."

Brad saw where this was going. "No way," he said. "We can't change Andre from an oversized racket to a mid-sized one. Not at this point. His serve might get faster, but he'll lose his touch everywhere else."

Andre agreed, of course. What do I know? But still I tried. "Andre," I said. "You're a pro. It'll take you a month to get used to the new racket. But without it, you'll *never* improve your serve."

He wouldn't listen to me.

In the fall of 1994, roughly when Andre won the U.S. Open for the first time, Pancho Gonzalez was diagnosed with cancer of the stomach, which had spread to his esophagus, chin, and brain. I can't say I was surprised; stomach cancer had killed his father 20 years earlier, and Pancho hadn't exactly been vigilant about his own health in the interim.

Over time, my attitude toward Pancho had softened somewhat. It takes a lot of energy to stay mad forever. Plus, Pancho had changed. He wasn't so prickly, so rude as before. The illness, the weakness it brought, made him much more humble. It was awful. Very difficult.

By the time he was diagnosed, Pancho and Rita had been divorced for five years or so. They'd given things their best shot, but Rita found out pretty quickly why Pancho had been divorced five times before he'd married her. I suppose Pancho himself put it best when he wrote in his autobiography, "A long time ago I came to the conclusion that I'm not composed of the stuff good husbands are made of." He became impossible to be around. He lost his job at Caesar's; I suspect he was just too proud to cater to the clientele.

Before they split, Pancho and Rita had a son, Skylar, who was born in 1985, but neither Rita nor Pancho were particularly adept at parenting. They just didn't know how to take care of the boy. Over time, the task of caring for Skylar fell to Betty. At first, she just babysat a lot, but eventually, we all gave up the charade and Skylar moved in with us. Fortunately, by then, Rita and I had begun to mend our relationship. Neither of us apologized or even discussed our grievance, but slowly, we naturally eased our way back to speaking terms.

That's not to say that Rita and Pancho didn't love Skylar. They did. Pancho, in particular, doted on the boy. Maybe it was because by the time Skylar was born, Pancho had retired from tennis and finally had the time to enjoy fatherhood — something he'd missed with his older children. Or maybe it was because when Skylar was a baby, he nearly drowned in Rita and Pancho's pool while Pancho, who was supposed to be watching him, slept. Rita came back from feeding the horses and found him at the bottom of the pool. She dove in, and saved him. Pancho had already lost one child, daughter Mariessa, who, at age 11, was thrown from a horse. He'd never been close to her, but her death had to have affected him. Either way, when Skylar pulled through, Pancho vowed to become a father in word *and* deed. Where Pancho was brash and rude to everyone else on the planet, he was patient and sweet with Skylar, and Skylar loved him right back.

Because we had custody of Skylar, we saw a lot of Pancho. He'd come over to pick him up, and he'd knock on the door. I'd open it and we'd talk. "How are you?" I'd say. "How is your health?" But he never came inside — except once, because he'd always wanted to see what Skylar's room looked like.

Coincidentally, I fell ill around the same time. In early 1995, I started having trouble breathing. Finally, I went to a cardiologist, who put me on a treadmill, gave me a cardiogram, and scheduled me for an angiogram.

Afterward, while I was waiting with Betty for the results, Phillip walked in.

"Dad," he said. "I don't want to freak you out or anything, but the doctor said that if you were his dad, he'd schedule you for heart surgery *tomorrow.*"

I looked at him, he looked at me. Finally, I spoke. "What? You want me to give you an answer? What do you want me to say?"

"I want you to say you'll have heart surgery tomorrow," Phillip shot back.

"I have to be mentally ready! I'm not ready!"

It was too much. Betty had just had gall-bladder surgery two weeks before; she could barely walk. I was too busy worrying about her to be able to start worrying about me. But eventually I got my head around it. I figured, if I die, I die. I put my affairs in order. I told Betty that if something happened to me, I wanted her to send $5,000 a year to my brother Helmut in Iran. As for the rest, she knew what to do.

I dreamt several nights that I was dead, in a casket. I was positive I wouldn't make it.

Except for Phillip, I'd been mum with my kids about my health situation. But of course, Phillip called Andre, who was in Palm Springs playing a tournament. Andre flew to Vegas to retrieve the test results, and then couriered them to some heart doctors in Texas.

"If that was your dad," he asked them, "where would you take him?"

Their answer: Dr. Lax at UCLA.

So Andre made a phone call, and then paid a visit to the doctor. Dr. Lax's day off was Tuesday, but Andre persuaded him to make an opening for me. I flew in on Monday, and on Tuesday I was under the knife for a quintuple bypass.

I survived, obviously, but Pancho wasn't so lucky. In typical Pancho fashion, he came out swinging against his cancer, but it was one opponent he could not beat. In June of 1995, yellow with illness,

Pancho checked into Sunrise Hospital. I visited him several times. He was in bad shape, but worse, he was embarrassed. He was embarrassed about his vulnerability. He'd been a legend, after all. More than that, though, he was embarrassed that he'd never been nice to the people who came to see him at the hospital. *Never.*

Pancho died on July 3, 1995. He was 67.

About 200 people came to Pancho's funeral — more than I expected, considering the way Pancho alienated just about everyone he ever met. Even his old rivals Rod Laver, Alex Olmedo, and Dennis Ralston came to pay their respects. The service was brief, as Pancho had intended. Afterward, we invited the mourners to our place and we fed them.

In 1996, Andre called home and told us he was planning to propose to Brooke.

He wasn't the first of my sons to get engaged. The year before, after nearly a decade of traveling with Andre, Phillip had married a lovely young woman named Marti and had settled in San Diego, where he'd found ample work as a tennis coach. They started a family a few years later, giving birth to a beautiful baby girl named Carter in 1998.

I'd had no objections to Phillip's wedding, but Andre's was another story.

"If that's what you want," I said, "you have my blessing." I wasn't happy about it, but then again, it wasn't my life. And who knew? Maybe I'd be proven wrong about Andre marrying Brooke, just as my mother had when I'd married Betty instead of a nice Armenian girl.

I doubted it.

The wedding was to be in Monterey on April 19, 1997, 10 days before Andre's 27th birthday. As the date neared, Betty flew out early to help; my plan was to arrive on the morning of the big day. On the day of my scheduled departure, I drove my car to the Tropicana, where I could park for free, and caught a cab the rest of the way to the airport. Somehow, between point A and point B, I lost my plane ticket and my wallet, which had a ream of cash in it. They must have fallen out of my pocket. All I had was my luggage and my car keys. I went back to my car and found some of my credit cards and my driver's license, but I was still missing my ticket.

Credit card in hand, I beelined back to the airport and bought a new ticket. But of course, by then, I'd missed my plane and had to wait for another. Finally, I arrived in Monterey, went to retrieve my luggage, and discovered that the plane's cargo door was jammed shut, making it impossible for the baggage handlers to remove our suitcases from the hold. Then, I found out that the limo that was supposed to pick me up had ditched when I hadn't showed up after my original flight's arrival.

It was not a good day.

By the time the wedding itself rolled around, the airlines had, fortunately, managed to pry open the plane and unload our bags, and mine had been delivered to the lodge that Andre and Brooke had rented out for the wedding. So after we got dressed, Betty and I found our way to the church and, with 150 other guests, sat for the service. We'd been told that the tabloids were willing to pay as much as $100,000 for exclusive photos — the day before, a photographer had disguised himself as shrubbery in order to sneak pictures at our hotel — so nobody but the official photographer was allowed to bring a camera into the chapel. The interior of the church was steaming hot; we'd closed the windows to block the noise of the paparazzi helicopters outside. When the ceremony was over, a 35-member boy's choir hollered an offbeat "Gloria," and we all piled into vans and made for the reception at the inn, followed by Andre and Brooke in a horse-drawn carriage.

At the reception, I sat down for dinner with my family — except for Andre, of course, who was with Brooke. We ate an obscenely expensive meal — a choice between veal scaloppini with mushroom risotto or chicken paillard with penne — and listened to toast after toast. After a while, I felt sick. Not sick physically, but sick. The stress of the day, my misgivings about Andre's marriage, it all rumbled in my gut like so much bad fish.

So I left.

In retrospect, I see that leaving your own son's wedding halfway through the reception isn't the greatest move a father could make. But I just had to get out of there, to breathe a bit. I think Andre viewed my early exit as some sort of protest statement, and maybe it was. I've never been great at hiding my feelings, especially when I see a problem. One thing I do know is Andre was terribly angry and hurt afterward, and I was sorry about that. Really I was. But it was done. I couldn't undo it.

Andre tanked in 1997.

He made the semis in San Jose, but skipped the Australian Open, the French Open, and Wimbledon, citing a wrist injury. (Brad Gilbert, however, attributed Andre's absence at Wimbledon to a lack of desire.) He lost in the first round in Memphis, Scottsdale, Indian

Wells, Key Biscayne, Washington, D.C., Los Angeles, Cincinnati, and Stuttgart. Things went a little better in Atlanta: There, he reached the *second* round. After making the quarters in Indianapolis, he woke up briefly for the U.S. Open, but was stopped in the fourth round by Patrick Rafter, who went on to win the title.

It didn't take a brain trust to figure out the problem: Andre was torn. He loved Brooke. He wanted to be with her. Chasing the tour meant spending weeks, even months apart. He just didn't want it. As for Brooke, she was busy with her show, with other acting jobs. She wasn't about to sacrifice that for Andre. After all, if history was any judge, she might never find work again. And so Andre made the sacrifices, following Brooke from location to location.

Andre, sometimes referred to as "Mr. Brooke Shields" by the press, was not happy. Worse, he was embarrassed, and more than a little angry. Andre knew that he had only a few more competitive years ahead of him — he figured five, tops — and he'd pretty much wasted this one.

Finally, after bottoming out at No. 141 (no, that's not a typo), Andre had had enough. With Brooke's blessing, he rededicated himself to tennis in late 1997. But by then, his confidence was so shattered, he opted to play the satellite circuit instead of the ATP tour. That way, he figured, he'd at least advance far enough in the brackets to get some playing time. Andre took a lot of guff for that in the press, but I was proud of him. A lesser man would have retired. In all truth, I thought it was time for him to just kiss it goodbye and start making appearances, playing exhibitions, that sort of thing. He was already set for life financially. He'd seen the No. 1 spot. He'd won a few Slams. He'd achieved everything I'd ever hoped for him. If he had quit, it would have been just fine with me.

But Andre had other ideas.

Through hard work, through steady effort, Andre turned things around in 1998. He didn't do much in the Slams, losing in the first round at Roland Garros, the second round at Wimbledon, and the fourth round in Australia and at Flushing Meadows. He did, however, win five tournaments: San Jose, Scottsdale, Washington, D.C., Los Angeles, and Ostrava. All told, after bottoming out in November the year before, Andre leapfrogged 137 slots in the rankings, ending the year at No. 4.

For Thanksgiving 1998, Andre invited all his friends and relatives to spend the holiday with him and Brooke in Malibu. The day before the big event, he stopped by the house.

"You coming to Malibu?" he said.

"I'm not coming."

I could tell he was frustrated. But you know, I was angry. He'd pulled away from us after marrying Brooke. He was so good to all his friends, but he never came to see us. He'd come to train with Gil on the court behind our house, or train in the gym next door, but he never bothered to walk over to our place, never bothered to visit his mother. Forget about me for a minute; what had Betty done to deserve that?

"What are you going to do," he said. "Sit in this big house all alone? Mom's coming to Malibu!"

I shot him a look, but didn't answer.

"Why won't you come?" he asked.

"I have to work," I said. It was true, I was scheduled to work, although we both knew I could have traded my shift if I'd wanted to.

So he left, and I spent the holiday on the casino floor.

I'd always been afraid something like this would happen to my family — indeed, it already had with Rita, although we were back on speaking terms by then — that we wouldn't talk, that we'd become strangers. The whole idea of a family at war was foreign to me. In Iran, my brothers and sister and parents had relied on each other to survive. We *had* to be close. But here in America, it wasn't like that — not for me, anyway. It hurt. It really hurt.

One night, in April of 1999, the phone rang. It was late. As always, Betty picked up.

It was Andre.

She listened, nodded as he spoke, and then hung up the phone.

"He's filing for divorce," she said, her eyes wide.

The next day, just 10 days shy of Andre and Brooke's two-year anniversary, it was final. Just like that.

Andre never told us what had happened, why he'd wanted a divorce, why he'd wanted it so quickly. I had a few suspicions; at my job, I occasionally heard things about Brooke that weren't exactly favorable, but I never passed those stories along to Andre. But whatever tipped Andre into the realm of reason, the fact that the couple had barely spent more than a week at a time together during the course of their almost-two-year marriage couldn't have helped matters much.

In any case, as far as I was concerned, the divorce was good news. Very good news. Especially since he was the one who broke things off.

Not long after the papers were filed, he called me.

"You were right," he said. He sounded sad. "You had the vision. I didn't have it. I didn't see clearly."

"I'm sorry," I said. I knew he was hurting. "I did know."

"But it's over now," he said. "It's done."

CHAPTER TEN

"To live in a family that really works, to be part of one that is always
there for you, and you for them, that does everything for each
other — I think that is very rare and very special."
— Steffi Graf

The 1999 French Open was significant in our lives for two
reasons.

One: Andre won it for the first time in his career. He'd reached
the finals twice before — in 1990 and 1991 — but, after winning the
first two sets, had folded each time. In 1999, however, Andre took a
different tack: *dropping* the first two sets to his opponent, Andrei
Medvedev, and charging back to win the match — his first Grand
Slam title since 1995.

I watched the game on TV, and I'll be honest, I never thought
he would win — especially after dropping those first two sets. I
knew his shoulder was bothering him, knew he was still a bit raw
from his divorce from Brooke, and I figured it just wasn't meant to
be. But win he did. Somehow, he put aside the pain, he dug deep
inside himself, and he triumphed. And in doing so, Andre became
only the fifth man ever (and only the second American) to win a
career Grand Slam — that is, win the Australian Open, the French

Open, Wimbledon, and the U.S. Open — officially marking his return to the highest echelons of men's tennis after tanking in the rankings in 1997.

Victory was sweet.

Two: At the victory dinner, a scant few weeks after divorcing Brooke, Andre summoned the courage to ask women's champion Steffi Graf on a date. Steffi herself was enjoying one hell of a comeback after reconstructive knee surgery in 1997; her win at Roland Garros over brat Martina Hingis was her first major since 1996.

As it turns out, it wasn't the first time Andre had asked Steffi out. Andre had admired Steffi from afar since 1992, when both won Wimbledon; they'd taken a picture together at the ball following the tournament. Soon thereafter, Andre persuaded his agent, Bill Shelton, to ask Steffi out on his behalf.

That time, Steffi said no.

Years later, when I found out Andre had enlisted Shelton to woo Steffi on his behalf, I told him he should have asked me to do it instead. I would have written her mom and dad and invited them all to dinner; Andre could have taken it from there. "That would have worked," Steffi told me, laughing.

Back in 1992, Steffi's impression of Andre was skewed by his spotty performance on the court, by his flamboyant clothes and hair — Andre probably wore nail polish more frequently than Steffi herself did — and by the fact that he was a born-again Christian. Steffi took Andre to be some sort of religious fanatic, and frankly, that just wasn't her thing. In fact, Andre *is* a born-again Christian. He became one not long after turning pro at a time when he felt lost and needed guidance. For Andre, Christianity offered peace of mind and the understanding that it's no big deal if you get beat. But unlike so many Christians, whose piety trumps any healthy mischief in their souls, Andre somehow strikes that delicate balance of being true to his god and true to himself. He doesn't temper his natural flamboyance, his outspoken nature, in the name of religion. He still swears and wears earrings. He's still Andre.

But after the 1999 French Open, when Andre tried his luck a second time — this time, having the good sense to ask her himself instead of sending his agent to do the job — Steffi saw him for the man he was, the man he had become, and said yes.

After that first date, Steffi severed her seven-year relationship with race-car driver Michael Bartels.

She and Andre were the real deal.

Like so many tennis players, Andre included, Steffi learned to play tennis from her father. But unlike many tennis players — Andre included — Steffi herself was the one who begged to be taught. And so, when Steffi turned four, her father, Peter, bought her a racket, sawed off the end to make it more manageable for Steffi's tiny hands, and drilled her on the fundamentals of the game. The pair volleyed over the living room couch for the ultimate prize: ice cream.

Before long, Peter began to suspect that Steffi might someday compete for a prize more valuable than dairy. Even as a toddler, Steffi was quick and coordinated, and could hit the ball squarely and with power. Peter began entering her in local tournaments and within a year, Steffi was hammering eight-year-olds off the court. She won her first junior tournament at age six.

Peter knew a prodigy when he saw one, so when he placed all his chips on his seven-year-old daughter — quitting his job as a used-car salesman in Mannheim, Germany, and moving the family to Bruhl, where he'd found a job as a teaching pro at a small tennis club in order to nurture Steffi's development — he knew his odds were good.

Needless to say, Peter's gamble paid off.

Steffi, so tiny you could barely see her over the net, claimed both the West German 14-and-under and 18-and-under titles at the tender age of 11. In 1982, Steffi, a precocious tow-headed 13-year-old with the strokes of an executioner, went pro. She played her first match against Tracy Austin. For three years, she traveled Europe's satellite circuit. In 1984, she won the gold medal at the Los Angeles Olympics (that year, tennis was a demonstration sport); she cracked the top 25 in 1985. In 1986, Steffi shot to No. 2 in the world. She won the French Open, her first Grand Slam singles title, in 1987, the same year she claimed the No. 1 ranking. She was 18.

Steffi's signature stroke, her forehand, was so powerful, she hit *so* hard, you half expected the ball to break down and name names. And although she was initially known to favor that shot, she quickly whittled her backhand and serve into equally sharp weapons. Combined with that quiver of deadly strokes was Steffi's incredible speed and athleticism; she was quick, she was agile.

In 1988, Steffi sacked and pillaged the tour. In addition to completing a career Grand Slam, Steffi won the gold medal at the Seoul Olympics, making her the first player, male or female, to win all five major titles in the same calendar year, a feat known as a "Golden Slam." In fact, Steffi was *so* dominant that reporters began asking the question on every other player's mind: When did she plan to retire? After all, what more could she possibly accomplish? Chris Evert told *Sports Illustrated* that the players all wished Steffi would fall in love, get married, and get pregnant. At least then someone else might have a shot at a major.

With Andre, Steffi would do all those things (though not quite in that order), but unfortunately for Evert, not for another decade. All told, during the course of her 17-year professional career, Steffi would seize an incredible 107 singles titles — including 22 Grand Slams — and roost atop the women's circuit for a record 377 weeks. If you were to graph Steffi's career, it would be, for the most part, as constant as pi.

Indeed, this incredible constancy *defined* Steffi. She was unswerving, terminally focused on the game. She was described as being as reliable as a German sewing machine — and about as interesting. As Andre's handlers perpetually sought to tone him down, to persuade him to focus on tennis, the opposite was true for Steffi: Her camp tried to make her seem more, well, human. "She likes to water ski!" they said. "She's quite into hiking!" "You should see her on a soccer field!" But their efforts were in vain. The truth was Steffi ate, slept, breathed tennis. Getting her to think about anything else was the rub.

All this time, I thought, so what if Steffi seemed to possess the personality of a librarian or had a grim demeanor as she dispatched opponent after opponent? So what if she didn't seem as feminine as Gabriela Sabatini or Chris Evert? (Of course, Steffi would later show us all just how gorgeously feminine she could be by posing for *Vogue* and for the *Sports Illustrated* swimsuit issue.) Steffi was winning. You had to appreciate *that*, at least. And the fact is, Steffi was a tremendously good sport. She'd question line calls even when doing so worked against her. She had tremendous class. Off the court, she was sweet and shy, sensitive, soft-spoken, humble, polite. *Normal.* So normal, in fact, that Steffi eschewed flashy endorsement contracts. Rather than promoting Mercedes Benz, Steffi endorsed the prosaic Opel. And Steffi and her family wisely maintained their old one-storey residence in the center of Bruhl instead of trading up to a home and location more befitting of Steffi's tax bracket (Monte Carlo, anyone?).

Unlike many families on the tour, the Grafs truly were close, truly took solace in each other. For Steffi, family was everything. She had few friends; because of her preoccupation with tennis, Steffi had been alternately teased and ignored in school, and any player will tell you that the women's tour isn't exactly a sisterhood. After each barb from the press about her robot-like play, about her prominent nose and her Teutonic shoulders, after each snide comment from other players, Steffi retreated deeper and deeper into the cocoon of her kin.

Although that cocoon was vigorously maintained by Steffi's mother, Heidi, who chaperoned Steffi on the tour (Steffi's younger brother, Michael, sometimes tagged along), it was Steffi's father who worked tirelessly to protect Steffi from the pitfalls, perils, and distractions that typically accompany tennis greatness, as well as the tremendous wealth that tennis greatness can generate. After Steffi went pro, Peter remained her coach in addition to adopting the duties of manager, handling Steffi's finances, hiring and firing additional coaches, limiting her playing time in an effort to stave off burnout, and shielding her from the prying eyes of the media to the extent it was possible. For her part, Steffi adored Peter, never resented his coaching, never bucked under his control. Theirs was a relationship of great, if rather unhealthy, symbiosis: Steffi was everything to Peter, and Peter was everything to Steffi.

Predictably, Peter's zeal to manage and protect Steffi fomented criticism. Peter, a.k.a. "Papa Merciless," was accused of manipulating Steffi's schedule to maintain her No. 1 ranking and of coaching her from the stands, which is, for some bizarre reason, as I learned when my kids were playing the junior circuit in Salt Lake City, not acceptable in tennis even though it is allowed in nearly every other sport on the planet. (Don't get me started.) He was known to hector officials and, on occasion, to bully fans who cheered Steffi's opponents. Journalists who criticized Steffi knew to expect an insulting response from Peter. He was called erratic, overbearing, abusive. He was, as tennis commentator Mary Carillo once put it, Steffi's "designated bastard." "The way Steffi is on the court," one family friend told *Sports Illustrated*, "that is Peter everywhere else."

Worse, like many Germans of his generation, Peter Graf was known to nurture a whopping persecution complex — though, in his case, he might have had good reason. It's well known that the Women's Tennis Association (WTA) gypped Steffi of more than a few matches — denying her access to a trainer for a knee injury in one, and allowing an opponent improper access to a trainer in another, among others. Worse, in 1988, as Steffi was on the brink of completing that Grand Slam, WTA officials were seen openly rooting *against* Steffi in the U.S. Open finals. As an aside, Steffi did not celebrate the night of her historic victory because Peter demanded that she fly immediately to Europe to attend to business there. Steffi was bitterly disappointed; it was one of the first and few times she resented her father's tight rein.

After a time, the paranoia, the stress, the money, the fame all got to Peter. He started drinking and taking pills. In 1990, when Steffi was 21, the German tabloid *Bild* revealed that a 22-year-old

Playboy Playmate had filed a paternity suit naming Peter Graf as the father of her infant daughter, and that Peter had paid the woman a considerable sum to withdraw it. Ironically, Peter's terrible betrayal mirrored one committed by his own father, except that Peter's father's actions drove Peter's mother to suicide. Peter never forgave him.

The news devastated Steffi. She had dealt with rain delays, even the occasional psychotic fan — one man slit his wrists on the Grafs' front stoop, in full view of Steffi — but Steffi's sheltered life hadn't prepared her for a distraction like the disintegration of her own family. Her confidence hobbled, Steffi snapped her 66-game winning streak by falling to 16-year-old newcomer Monica Seles at the German Open. Her losing ways continued at the French Open — again, Steffi fell to Seles — and at Wimbledon. Mr. and Mrs. Graf did make up — they were seen holding hands at the All England Lawn Tennis & Croquet Club — but for Steffi, the damage had been done. Her on-court woes continued as Monica Seles's star rose; Seles went on to win seven of the next 11 Grand Slam singles titles, stripping Steffi of her No. 1 ranking.

At this, the first blip on the graph of Steffi's career, the whispers started: Was Steffi, at 23, washed up?

On April 30, 1993, the day after Andre's 23rd birthday, a spectator stabbed Monica Seles during a changeover at a tournament in Germany. I was watching the match on TV. She was sitting there, minding her own business, when all of a sudden this guy puts a knife in her back. As she fell to the court, several spectators wrestled the man to the ground.

I was shocked.

It was quickly revealed that the perpetrator, Günther Parche, was a deranged fan of Steffi's, that he had stabbed Monica for usurping Steffi's No. 1 ranking.

Steffi was horrified.

She felt guilty, I'm sure, and terribly sorry. But I think Steffi just wasn't that good at talking about her feelings back then. She didn't know what to say, how to react. So she did what she'd always done: retreated into her family, into herself, into tennis. And with Monica out, Günther Parche got his wish: Steffi quickly reclaimed the No. 1 ranking. There was talk, at the time, of allowing Monica to remain No. 1 until she returned to the tour, but the players struck this down. Monica's fans excoriated Steffi for staying mum on the issue; I suspect Steffi just didn't know what to say or do. But for Steffi, it was terrible knowing that she was No. 1 because Monica had been attacked. And she missed having a rival, a challenger, on the tour.

That year, she won 10 tournaments.

Despite her success, a darkness settled over Steffi. She was like a soldier, returned from a long and unspeakable war. She curled up into herself. She began traveling less with her family, spending more time on her own. Where before she had been described as "shy" or "quiet," she was now called "rude." The press called her "Little Miss Sour Kraut." She considered retiring, but she played on, claiming seven titles in 1994. She didn't know what else to do.

Just when it looked like things couldn't get worse for Steffi, they did.

In August 1995, the German government arrested and imprisoned Steffi's father, accusing him of funneling millions of marks — *Steffi's* marks — to offshore tax havens. He had filed no tax forms for Steffi during the years 1989 to 1992, instead paying lump sums amounting to at most 10 percent of Steffi's income — far below Germany's obscene 56-percent top tax rate. The family's tax adviser soon joined Peter in jail. Steffi herself endured multiple interrogations by German officials, though she, of course, knew nothing about her finances. She was a tennis player, not an accountant.

Needless to say, the media went nuts over the story. They followed her everywhere, camping out on her doorstep in Bruhl, outside her SoHo apartment in New York. The German press was especially egregious, reporting on private conversations between Steffi and Peter during supervised visits and on letters sent to Peter by Heidi. *Bild*, the German tabloid, excerpted Peter's confidential psychiatric profile. And of course, everywhere there was talk about Steffi's culpability: *She knew. Of course she knew. If she didn't know, then she should have!* This talk, despite Peter's — and the family's accountant's — firm statements to the contrary.

Even winning the 1995 U.S. Open, against none other than Monica Seles in her triumphant comeback year, wasn't enough to steer the conversation back to tennis. In the press conference after her victory in the finals, when asked when she would next see her father, Steffi burst into tears and bolted from the room.

The bad news just kept coming. A reeling Steffi began experiencing chronic back problems. She had surgery to remove a painful bone spur from her left foot. Her favorite dog died. After a five-month trial, Peter was convicted in early 1997 and sentenced to three years and nine months. Her parents split up.

But some good things happened too: Steffi was struck by the new compassion of her fans, who had finally glimpsed Steffi's sensitivity, her vulnerability, her deep humanity. She began taking control of her finances and of her life. She hired a staff, set up an office, and formed her own sports-promotion company. In 1995 and 1996, she won the French Open, Wimbledon, and the U.S. Open. Even better, Steffi began to appreciate tennis in a new way; the game became a much-needed respite from the troubles that plagued her personal life. "There is so much joy in being on the court and winning when it is so much more difficult because of all the circumstances," she told *Sports Illustrated* in November 1996. "I treasure these moments so much more than I ever did."

Through it all, Steffi never turned her back on Peter, and I respected her for that. "When you know what alcohol and tablets can do to you," she told *Sports Illustrated*, "it's difficult to be angry." She continued, "I love him dearly. Nothing in that department will change. He needs help. He will need a lot of help. I know what's ahead of me."

But the gods weren't finished testing Steffi yet. After a tournament in late 1996, Steffi began experiencing knee problems. She played through the pain until it grew so intense, she could barely move. After losing to Amanda Coetzer in the quarterfinals of the 1997 French Open, Steffi underwent surgery on her left knee to repair a ruptured patellar tendon and cartilage tears. The surgeons offered no guarantees; she'd probably be able to walk okay, but beyond that, all bets were off.

Steffi approached her rehab with characteristic intensity and determination, and after eight months away from the WTA tour, Steffi, whose ranking bottomed out at No. 91 in the world, tentatively returned to tennis. She didn't expect to dominate the game as she once had — really, she didn't expect much at all. She just wanted to play for as long as she liked and to end her career on her own terms.

Initially, Steffi's comeback was hampered by minor injuries. A hamstring pull sidelined her at the semis at Indian Wells. The three screws in her knee bothered her, and in compensating for that, she strained her calf. Her wrist required minor surgery. She had a foot injury. She was disappointed at Wimbledon and the U.S. Open, losing in the third and fourth rounds, respectively, but she reached the quarters in Hannover and Eastbourne, the semis in Birmingham, and claimed titles in New Haven, Leipzig, and Philadelphia.

In the end, no one was particularly surprised by Steffi's comeback. When you've had results like Steffi's, no one should ever count you out. But Steffi herself was surprised by how warmly she was received. During her introduction at her first tournament back, the crowd's cheers swelled to a spontaneous tribute, a standing ovation; flabbergasted by the rush of affection, Steffi broke down and wept. Steffi, the woman who had stoically borne the loneliness of life on tour, the scandals of her father, the dissolution of her family, the attempted murder of her rival, debilitating back pain, and a ruined knee, finally wept.

Interestingly, Steffi's comeback coincided with Andre's resurrection in the rankings, and I suspect that's when her opinion of him began to change. She hated that Andre was thumped in the press and by other players for battling his way through the satellites, and loved it each time he proved himself. As for Andre, he could relate to the frustration of being dismissed as a has-been, the way Martina Hingis cattily suggested that not only was Steffi too old to win again, but that the game itself had advanced beyond Steffi's capabilities.

Steffi's response: To tear Hingis apart in the finals of the French Open in 1999, to declare it the greatest win of her career, to agree to a date with Andre, and to end her relationship with Michael Bartels.

Incredibly, Andre and Steffi kept their bond a secret at Wimbledon, where both reached the finals. (Andre lost to Sampras, and Steffi lost to Lindsay Davenport. For her part, Hingis lost in the first round.) Their growing relationship remained a secret still at the U.S. Open, which Steffi declined to enter, and which Andre won, besting Todd Martin in five sets.

It was a secret, even from us, until Brooke Shields called us to break the news. Betty picked up.

"Do you know who Andre's been seeing?" Brooke asked.

"No," said Betty. "Who?"

"Steffi Graf!" Brooke exclaimed, incredulous. Maybe it was hard for Brooke to believe a man could prefer a woman like Steffi to someone like her.

As for me, I was pleased to find out they'd connected. I didn't know Steffi well, but I had a good impression of her. Anytime I saw her around, she was always nice, always polite, and her parents were too.

"They're both from the same stable," I told Betty, and she agreed.

It's easy for a guy like me to understand why Andre would be crazy about Steffi: She's a lot like my Betty. She's low maintenance, kind, easy-going. Plus, once, when asked which celebrity she'd been most excited to meet, she didn't say Madonna or Michael Jordan or Harrison Ford. No, Steffi's answer was Max Schmeling, the great German boxer who had defied and confounded Adolph Hitler by continuing to consort with Jews and, later, by merely staying alive all those years ago. I mean, who *wouldn't* love this girl?

The best thing about Steffi, though, is that she's very family oriented. She'd received so much love and support from her own family over the years, she just can't help it. In fact, Steffi is so family oriented she even managed to bring *our* family back together. Anyone who's Andre's relative, she treats as her own.

The fact is, at the time Andre and Steffi started dating, my own relationship with Andre was still a bit strained. The end of his marriage with Brooke had at least opened the door, but for the most part, we both stayed clear of the threshold.

Steffi changed all that. Steffi made him come around.

One day, she just showed up at the house, all by herself. She hugged me, kissed my cheek, and asked how I was doing.

"Fine," I said. I invited her inside, we sat down, and we talked. I don't even remember what we talked about; that wasn't important. I just thought it was nice of her to reach out.

She did that several times, just dropped by, and eventually she started bringing Andre. And after a while, he just eased back into our lives.

I give credit to Steffi. She saw that our family was broken, and she knew just what to do to fix us.

CHAPTER ELEVEN

"Until I saw my sister and mother battling cancer,
I didn't know what it meant to be a fighter."
— Andre Agassi

Right around the time that Andre won the Australian Open for the second time, in January of 2000, my daughter Tami found a lump the size of a marble during a routine breast exam. She was alarmed, of course, but then again, she was only 30. She was healthy and fit. There was no history of breast cancer in the family. At the time, the chances of a woman 30 or under getting the disease were 1 in 2,525, and anyone who's ever been to Vegas can tell you those were good odds. Besides, Tami was busy with her new dot-com job — back when there *were* dot-com jobs — in Seattle. So she waited a few weeks before having it checked out.

Finally, she went to the doctor and had a mammogram and an ultrasound.

"It's a tumor," the radiologist said. "But there's a 98 percent chance it's benign."

They told her she could have it biopsied or removed, but neither the radiologist nor Tami's doctor seemed particularly concerned.

But Tami was. The way she put it, there was something in her that hadn't been there before, and she wanted to find out what the hell it was. So Tami got a second opinion, this time from a specialist.

His take: The lump was almost certainly cancerous, and required immediate removal.

Tami didn't tell the family right away. She wanted to have all the facts first, so we wouldn't freak out. But she did call Rita to ask about a friend who'd had a breast removed. She didn't tell Rita why she was asking, but Rita's no fool. She was onto Tami immediately. Pretty soon, we all were, and it frightened us. Tami was too young. The thought of there being any disease in her body . . . well, it was too horrible to ponder. We just couldn't imagine how something like this could happen to our Tami.

In our family, Tami is the glue. She's the one who keeps us all together. She's the peacekeeper, the busybody, and she knows what everyone is doing. She watches out for us. Phillip might get mad at Rita, Rita might get mad at Andre, Andre might get mad at me, but *nobody* gets mad at Tami. Ever. She's close with everyone. If anything happened to Tami, I just don't know how we'd all cope. As for me, I don't have a favorite kid. All four of them are fantastic, each in his or her own way. But Tami's the one who's the sweetest on me. She tends to cut me a break whenever I piss off Rita, Phillip, and Andre — which, over the years, has been rather often.

Even though Andre was in Zimbabwe playing Davis Cup when he got the news, he scrambled to find Tami the best medical care money could buy, just as he'd done for me when I'd needed heart surgery five years earlier. But Tami was satisfied with the top-notch oncologist who had diagnosed her condition. Besides, she wanted to stay in Seattle. Her life was there. It was her home.

Betty was the one who christened Tami, and she chose the name

— Tamara, Tami for short — because she thought it was sporty, spunky, and that's just how Tami turned out to be. So it surprised no one when she came out swinging against cancer. Her first step was to educate herself about the disease. She read everything she could get her hands on. And when it came time to decide her course of treatment, Tami opted for the most aggressive route. Even though cancer had been found in only one breast and the odds weren't particularly high that it would occur in the other, she had a double mastectomy. She knew that having a double mastectomy wouldn't kill her, but having cancer would. It was her way of playing the odds.

We flew to Seattle immediately to be with Tami during her surgery, and we stayed for about a month afterward to keep her company and make sure she had everything she needed. Afterward, Tami took a leave of absence from her job and underwent chemotherapy for nine months. She was exhausted all the time, but she toughed it out, and eventually, she kicked the disease.

I don't mean to say that if someone diagnosed with breast cancer just does what Tami did, she can be cured. Just like you can whale away at a boxer in the ring and still lose a bout, you can come out with the big guns in cancer and lose the battle. Life's just unfair that way. But I do think that what Tami did — educating herself, opting for the most aggressive treatment — gave her a fighting chance. I was proud of how she handled herself in the face of such devastating news. I was proud of her strength, her toughness, through it all.

Hell, all my kids handled themselves during Tami's illness about as well as a guy could reasonably hope. Rita, who, with a bum thyroid, suffered her own share of health problems that year, was a rock for Tami emotionally. Andre bought her a house so she wouldn't have to worry about living expenses during her leave of absence from work. When the chemo started making Tami's hair fall out in clumps, Andre, himself no stranger to hair woes, went to work on her with his clippers in a ceremonial shearing. When he was finished, Andre and Phillip disappeared into the bathroom, emerging moments later with totally bald heads, shaved in a show of support.

About seven months after Tami's breast cancer diagnosis, in August of 2000, one of Betty's breasts became infected. It had swelled up and was unbearably tender. When Tami got wind of that, she called Phillip and asked him to make sure Betty got taken to the doctor, told him to make sure all the hard questions got asked. I felt certain that Betty was fine — she'd had a mammogram the year before that had come back clean — but after what we'd been through with Tami, we figured a visit to the doctor couldn't hurt, so we went.

Betty's doctor took one look at that breast and relayed her to a specialist, who gave her a mammogram.

She had cancer. The infection was a result of a mass in her breast. The specialist compared the mammogram with the one from the previous year and found that the mass had been present then, too, but whoever read that earlier mammogram hadn't noticed it. She'd been walking around with breast cancer the entire time Tami had been undergoing treatment! The verdict: Betty needed a mastectomy . . . and fast.

Well, after what we'd been through with Tami, this was just too much. The kids were a mess. Betty, well, she's *Betty*. She is the heart of this family. I might have been the driving force behind my kids' success with tennis, but Betty's the one who showed them how to live and how to love. She is kind. She is patient. Betty never cared whether Rita or Phillip or Tami or Andre lost a tennis match; they always knew she loved them just the same. Even when I went years without speaking to Rita and Andre, they always called home to catch up with Betty. For the kids, Betty is . . . well, she's their mother. She's their *home*.

We all worried how Betty's illness would affect Tami, but she hung tough. Even the weakness caused by her own chemo couldn't keep Tami away. She hopped on a plane from Seattle to be by Betty's bedside practically the minute she heard the news. Phillip and Rita, too. As for Andre, he found out just before the U.S. Open. He won his first-round match, but in the second round, decided to shank and fly home. A few days later, sensing the long road ahead, he formally withdrew from the U.S. Olympic tennis team, which was bound for the Sydney Olympiad in September.

Andre's not afraid to throw a match in a crisis. At the 2001 French Open, after the first set of his quarterfinal match against Sebastien Grosjean, Andre received word that a longtime employee of his was very near to succumbing after a long battle with cancer. The prognosis: The woman had, at best, 24 hours to live. This was someone who had been with Andre for years, and for him, it was more important to get home to sit with her in her last hours than it was to play out the match. And so, after winning the first set 6–1, Andre blew the next three. The funny thing was, everyone thought it was because Bill Clinton had been in the audience, that the presence of the former President jangled Andre's nerves, but that wasn't it at all. Anytime Andre loses early in a tournament like that, chances are there's a good reason for it.

For her part, Betty kept her cool. Maybe it was because she'd just seen Tami go through the same thing, so she knew what to expect. Absolutely, it was because of the support she received from the kids. The surgery was tough on her physically, but mentally she kept it together, even when she started hemorrhaging a week later. After I came home from work to find her bleeding, I rushed her to the emergency room. They tried to just give us a towel to stem the bleeding and send us home, but I said to the nurse, "Look, she is in pain. Can you at least give her some kind of shot?"

The doctor came in with some kind of hypodermic, flicked it a few times, and then barked at Betty, "Roll over!"

Poor Betty, she couldn't roll over. She couldn't move at all!

Anyway, finally, they got everything worked out, and she was fine. She lost a lot of blood, but she was fine.

The way Betty saw things, she'd had a good life. Whatever happened, happened. She was of an age, 63 at the time, where she could live with dying if that was in the cards. She'd done everything she'd ever wanted to do — raised a family, had a good job. She had no regrets.

She was very brave.

As for me, I just prayed she'd get well. I thought, Tami made it through, Betty would too. I just didn't permit myself to imagine a life without Betty. In the end, my prayers were answered. Betty's mastectomy did the trick; she required no additional treatment and was back to normal within a year or so.

It's funny how life is. By the time Tami and Betty got sick, it wasn't like we all still *hated* each other. A lot of the fences in our family had been mended. Over the years, Rita and I had gotten our act together; gone were the days when we'd pass each other without speaking. And thanks to Steffi, Andre was back in the fold. I'd talk to the kids every so often; they no longer had a policy against dealing with me. Nevertheless, we weren't part of each others' daily lives.

After the cancer, things changed. We became more sociable. We talked more. We became part of each others' daily lives. And in doing so, after all these years, we discovered just what it means to be a family.

CHAPTER TWELVE

"It is in the love of one's family only that heartfelt happiness is known."
— Thomas Jefferson

Here's what a typical day is like for me:

I wake up around 7:00 a.m., and tinker around the house for a while. If I feel like it, I climb into the buff-colored Cadillac that Andre bought me a few years back and putt over to the Omelet House, a hole-in-the-wall diner on Charleston Boulevard that's been in Las Vegas almost as long as I have. If she feels like it, Betty will come with me. I'll kid around with the waitresses, order my breakfast — an omelet, white toast, black coffee.

Afterward, when we get home, I might crank up the ball machines on the tennis court out back and hit around for a while.

If it's a weekend, you can bet the phone will be ringing off the hook. Tami and Rita always call to talk to Betty. Phillip is in the mix, too, but he's not quite as communicative as the girls. He still lives in San Diego with his wife, Marti, and his daughter, Carter, who is beautiful and very clever. Rita lives here in Vegas; she teaches tennis, and has recently begun studying psychology at UNLV. She's strong and she's smart and she's tough, and she still has one hell of a forehand. As for Tami, she's still in Seattle, where she works for the oncologist who monitored her treatment, Dr. Saul Rivkin, raising money for cancer research.

The way I see it, now that Tami's on the job, the disease doesn't stand a chance.

Tami is seeing an interesting guy. His name is Lobsang — I call him "Lobster" just to tease him. He was born a goatherder in Tibet. When he was 13, his parents sent him to a Buddhist monastery. At 19, he walked more than 4,500 kilometers, crossing the Himalayas, to India, where he became a monk under the tutelage of the Dalai Lama. (And Andre thought *he* had it bad; at least he didn't have to walk to Bradenton when we sent him to Bollettieri's academy!) Eventually, after many years of study — he became an expert in five religions and eight languages — he moved to New York and then to Seattle, arriving with only $480 in his pocket. He spoke no English, but given his propensity for languages, he quickly learned. Lobsang began working for Sprint Corporation, and within two years became the No. 11 salesman in the company. Since then, he's become the founder and CEO of his own software business. If you're smart, you'll stop reading this book right now and see if you can buy or borrow one about Lobsang. If there's not one yet, there will be — or at least, there *should* be.

I suppose Tami and Lobsang will probably get married, and that's okay with me. It doesn't really matter to me who she picks. She's got a brain in her head. We trust her to make a good decision.

Both Tami and Betty are 100 percent cancer free.

If Andre and Steffi are in town, they'll usually drop by. Unless you've spent the last several years living in an Afghan cave, you probably know that after more than two years of dating, Andre married Steffi at their home on October 22, 2001. It was a private ceremony, even more private than mine and Betty's. In addition to a district judge, who performed the nuptials, only Betty and Steffi's mother, Heidi, who had moved to Las Vegas by then, were there. I didn't even know about it until after it was over! I came home from work, and Betty, all smiles, let me in on the secret. I was sorry to have missed the show, but I have no hard feelings. After all, Andre wasn't invited to my wedding either.

Four days after the wedding, their first child, Jaden, was born. It's an odd name, but both Steffi and Andre liked it. It means "God has heard" in Hebrew, and I guess He has. He has heard us all, I think. On October 3, 2003, Andre and Steffi were blessed again, this time with the birth of a beautiful baby girl, who they named Jaz.

Skylar still lives with us. Skylar's all grown up now — 18 years old, a giant kid, well over six feet tall, with the dark good looks of his father. Given who his parents are, Skylar can't escape being a decent tennis player (he has one hell of a serve), but because of his size, baseball should be his game.

Jaden adores Skylar, so as soon as Jaden careens through our front door, he's off to the races, hunting Skylar down. When Jaden finds him, Skylar can be counted on for at least one good wrestling match. They'll roll around on the floor for a time while Andre, Steffi, and Betty, who take turns playing with little Jaz, cheer them on. Steffi or Andre usually hits around for a while on the court out back, and sometimes I join in. Before they leave, Jaden will inevitably ask if he can give the dog a treat, so I'll pull some Milk Bones from the pantry, and he'll carefully place one on the floor.

I suspect that Steffi and Andre won't foist tennis on their children, but I do know they've started teaching Jaden how to play, and I bet Jaz won't be far behind. With genes like that, it'd be a crime not to. A few months ago, Jaden hit the ball from the baseline over the net for the first time, so I'd say the kid has promise.

After the kids and grandkids leave and things quiet down, if there's a good match on television, I'll settle in to watch it using the special remote control that Steffi bought me one year after picking my name in the family Christmas gift draw. It was a great gift! It allows me to manage signals from multiple sources from one device. I cross my fingers every year that she'll draw my name again. Each match I watch proves that tennis has changed in all the ways I thought it would: It's faster; the players hit the ball harder, on the rise; serve-and-volley has become an effective style; and the money is huge — though, due to the general incompetence of tennis' governing bodies, interest in the game has declined.

Eventually, mid-afternoon, I'll put on my suit and head over to the casino for work, driving the back way to avoid as much traffic as possible. We've lived in Vegas long enough that the Strip doesn't hold much allure beyond providing a paycheck.

I work at the MGM Grand now. People ask me, "Do you think you'll ever retire?" I say, "Yeah. I retire every day." My job's so great, that's what it feels like anyway. Basically, I'm a host, a greeter. I walk all over the casino and dining room, greeting our guests. I can stop anyone I see and start a conversation. In fact, I'm *required* to. I guess I'm what you'd call "local color." Being Andre's father helps; I swear, 50 percent of the people who go in that place either know me or know *of* me. They're happy to meet me, and I'm happy to meet them, too. A lot of times I get asked for Andre's picture or his auto-graph, and I try to accommodate people whenever I can.

At the end of each shift, I hope I've done something positive for MGM because the MGM Grand has done so many positive things for me. In all, I've worked there for more than 20 years.

Maybe my job's so cushy because I've known the owner, the legendary Kirk Kerkorian, since 1963; we met not long after I arrived in Vegas, and have been friends for more than 40 years. In fact, Andre's middle name is Kirk, and Kerkorian is the reason why. Kirk is Armenian, like I am, and a tennis player. Besides, he's fond of my son. Plus, my bosses like me, and as long as they don't tell me to stay home, I'll keep coming to work each day.

Speaking of retiring, I'm guessing Andre won't either. He'll quit tennis, of course, though I wouldn't dare speculate when. I will say, though, that if I live again, I'll teach my kids golf. Golf you can play for a lifetime. Tennis, not so much. But I figure as long as Andre feels like he can compete on the court, he'll continue to do so, and so far, he's remained competitive. He won the Australian Open in 2001 and again in 2003. In the summer of 2003, he reclaimed the No. 1 spot for a time — at 33, the oldest man to do so in the Open era. In fact, I contend that if, through some miracle of science, you could pit 2004 Andre against 1992 Andre, 1992 Andre would get his clock cleaned. Andre hasn't lost a step, hasn't lost one joule of power, and at the same time has improved his fitness and mental game immeasurably.

Although Andre continues to work with Gil Reyes, his strength coach, Andre and Brad Gilbert parted ways in early 2002. No reason, really, except that both were ready to move on. Gilbert coaches Andy Roddick now, and Andre has teamed up with Darren Cahill, who was credited with coaching Lleyton Hewitt to a U.S. Open title and a No. 1 ranking in 2001. I am happy to report that Cahill listened to my pitch to change Andre's strings, and Andre has switched to a racket that is marginally smaller — though not as small as I'd like.

It's getting harder, though. Not the playing; Andre's game is better than ever. What's hard now is leaving Steffi, leaving the kids. He longs to be with them, and they with him.

When he does hang it up on the tour, Andre won't be one of those athletes who can't figure out what to do next. He'll do appearances and play exhibitions, of course, but he's got more than that on his plate. He's signed on to develop a fitness center. He's got a stake in the Golden Nugget casino. He's backing a bar being built in front of Caesar's Palace. He owns a surf-and-turf restaurant in Las Vegas, called Sedona, which is meant to be the first of a chain. It's odd, when you think about it: I've worked in the hospitality industry — in hotels, restaurants, casinos — my whole career, and now Andre will too. I'm sure he'll stay on with a lot of his sponsors — Canon, Head, Gillette, Nike. And of course, he's extremely devoted to his charity, the Andre Agassi Charitable Foundation. Andre knows that it was the generosity of others that put food on our table; I worked in showrooms for tips, after all. So it's very important to him to spread the wealth.

A few years back, the foundation funded the construction of the Andre Agassi Boy's and Girl's Club of Las Vegas. It also backs the Andre Agassi College Preparatory Academy, a charter school for underprivileged children where at-risk kids receive an education on par with the best private schools, tuition-free. A school! This from the guy who dropped out of high school to play tennis. He did earn his diploma through correspondence courses, but you see my point. Then again, maybe it's not so surprising after all. Education might not have been a priority for Andre as a young person, but he *is* one of the smartest guys I know.

So in short, he'll be fine.

And as long as Andre's doing fine, everybody's happy.

It's funny the way history repeats itself. Just as I took care of my parents and my siblings in Iran after moving to America, Andre helps all of us. He's generous. All my kids are. A lot of people would give their right arm to have kids like mine. Andre bought our house, our cars. He bought a condo for Rita, a house for Tami. He pays Phillip a monthly salary to work for his company, Agassi Enterprises. He covers Skylar's school expenses, plus his clothes, his car, and his pocket money. All of us, all our lives are better because of Andre.

And maybe, just maybe, Andre's life and the lives of all my children are good, at least in part, because of me.